DEDICATION

As a salute to your inner guide, this book is dedicated to the treasured light within you.

"... For this cause I was born, and for this cause I have come into the world, that I should bear witness to the truth ..."

(John 18:37 NKJV)

RADIATING
RENEWED
LIGHT

EFFECTIVELY USING THE POWER OF
SEEKING TO ACTIVATE
TRANSFORMATIONAL ENERGY FOR
LIVING MORE ABUNDANTLY

KALI DENISE

Radiating Renewed Light
Effectively Using the Power of Seeking to Activate Transformational
Energy for Living More Abundantly

For permission requests, speaking inquiries, and bulk order
purchase options, email iamintentiontuned@gmail.com

ISBN: 979-8-9928630-7-9

Book Design by Transcendent Publishing
Edited By Shelby Rawson

Disclaimer: This publication is designed to provide general
information regarding the subject matter covered. While the author
has used their best efforts in preparing this book, the author in no
way, shape, or form considers any of the information in this book to
be advice, promise, guarantee, warranty, or any form of professional
advice. You should conduct your own research to verify all
information or seek a professional's opinion when appropriate.
Neither the publisher nor the author shall be liable for any results.

TABLE OF CONTENTS

This book can be read in any order, although reading in order by chapter sheds light on the following context. The table of contents can be used as a checklist.

ACKNOWLEDGMENT

I hereby acknowledge that what I am writing to you is directly inspired by Light. May all the glory be to God.

"If anyone thinks they are a prophet or otherwise gifted by the Spirit, let them acknowledge that what I am writing to you is the Lord's command." (1 Corinthians 14:37 NIV)

MESSAGE FROM THE AUTHOR

We are part of the sun's solar system. We are within it, and the sun's energy is within us. As solar-powered beings, hybrids of matter and energy, we are the light of the world.

As I paid more attention to the highest power, I began to identify more as a spiritual being. As the light, I could no longer disregard the sun of God. Signs of God are emitted by all light sources. I became aware of my inseparable connection to the intense light above. I started recognizing the power of the sun's spirit. Since then, God's sun and I have exchanged many messages about its strength to renew the mind and heal the body. This book is a result of our conversations.

When I initially started writing, my work was intended as a tool for my personal use. The idea was to create visuals and a brief descriptive text to help me understand the spiritual work I sensed was about to commence. When I completed the manuscript for this book and was drafting the intro, I reviewed the initial drafts of my work. On the first page in large bold text, it stated:

"Who are you, and why are you here?"

My initial drafts were an eight-page illustrative document, in which I attempted to answer the question above. In large bold text, as the header of the following seven pages, it stated:

"I AM ..."

This is how I conceived the content of this book. This question to myself obviously took me on a journey. As you process the content on the following pages, you will also be taken on a journey to a place where only you can go. This book unites pertinent scientific concepts, Biblical text, and my direct experience with the effects of light's energy.

This literary work isn't about becoming. It's a reminder that you already have the power to be, do, have, and feel all that you desire. It serves as a spiritual spark along your path towards the continuous unveiling of inherited truth that already resides within you. This is an energy interaction of two souls linked by a spiritual connection.

May the reaction of your spirit to this content be so empowering that you receive energy restoration which penetrates to the deepest levels of your being to liberate your soul, renew your mind, and heal your body. May you continue to be filled with positive light as you gain the strength to conquer all obstacles.

Almost ten years prior to writing this book, it became apparent that I had reached the invisible ceiling created by the limitations of my own mind. I intuitively knew the only way to surpass it was to unveil the inherited truth within myself.

I realized the superpower of overcoming the world was obtained by intentionally redirecting my mind away from external distractions to focus on strengthening my inner light. Turns out, this simple strategy is easier said than done when constantly stimulated by reality and strongly identifying as my physical characteristic.

Something within me shifted a year before starting this book. Now I'm willing to travel wherever my inner guide leads. I wholeheartedly live for this journey. On the following pages, I share the concepts that I used to disregard the fear of embracing my authentic nature to live as my higher self.

All the things you do for the sake of healing, peace, transformation, activation, harmony, letting go, alignment, enlightenment, grounding, ascending, and reprogramming are beneficial to your journey. However, the simple truth is within you. Your way is the way. The interactions along your unique path activate the spiritual current within you for continuous movement towards your intended direction. This is the flow of nature.

"Do not remember the former things, Nor consider the things of old. Behold, I will do a new thing, Now it shall spring forth; Shall you not know it? I will even make a road in the wilderness And rivers in the desert." (Isaiah 43:18-19 NKJV)

PART I

THE SPIRIT OF ALL THINGS

CHAPTER 1

THE FORGOTTEN FREQUENCY

Born to Radiate Loving Light

Imagine your initial perception of consciousness occurring while you are within the limitless energy field of heaven. You are surrounded by bright white light that begins to fade into darkness. Simultaneously, shining starlights start to appear in the distance surrounding you. Then you begin descending towards Earth and into your mother's womb.

As you approach your destination, your surroundings seem to start contracting. While in heaven you were tuned to the pure frequency of God's love, the highest power. Your eternal soul still has the impressions and memories of this frequency. Upon exiting the womb for delivery, your natural high from heaven continues to dissipate.

You've entered the world that instantly begins to drain your energy, lowering your vibrational frequency. The lower your energy, the further away you are from God's frequency. With every dose of reality, the memories of your soul and awareness of your spiritual connection quickly dissolve like a dream upon awakening. You become reprogrammed by the experiences of your new atmosphere. The physical body you have inhabited now seems to be all that you are. The delusion of your identity begins.

Along the journey of life, something within you becomes activated by a divinely orchestrated set of events. You have a sense that there is a priceless treasure to be discovered within you. You have detected the most powerful energy source. Occasionally, you tap into the heavens you once knew. These moments elevate your consciousness like nothing you've ever experienced. The glimpses of greatness have motivated you to start a practice of seeking within yourself. The Spirit within you is the energy source that your soul has been longing to consciously reconnect with.

Your hectic lifestyle causes you to occasionally lose focus. Today, you're ready to regain your focus with an unwavering commitment. Your energy system is ready to perform, powered by the vibrational frequency of life-giving light in all aspects of your life. This is a gradual process. You have always been interconnected to the ultimate energy source. You simply forgot your way home or have become too distracted to harness the full potential of your light.

> *"Awake, you who sleep, Arise from the dead, And Christ will give you light." (Ephesians 5:14 NKJV)*

KEYNOTES | THE FORGOTTEN FREQUENCY

Spiritual awareness involves being conscious of your role as Director of Energy for your system. Regaining an awareness of your relation to heavenly power or cosmic light can trigger an impulse to learn more about the attributes of light's effects in your life. Not only are you within the field of cosmic light, but it is also within you. The light from above is absorbed by you and reflects off you, providing the spirit to be who you are and for you to be seen.

When the weight of the world seems to pull you down, you can remember that you descended from the heavens above and are predestined to continuously rise. The experience on Earth is simply determined by your viewpoint. The view from Earth's surface is designed to show that even the brightest star has a continuous cycle of ups and downs. When the sun appears to be down, the light is still brightly shining. All stars eventually burn out, but they are created to rise and shine until then.

Spiritual Spark Exercise

Think back to when you first realized you were on a spiritual journey. Take a moment to appreciate how far you've come and the positive changes you've made since then.

CHAPTER 2

YOU ARE THE LIGHT OF THE WORLD

About Your Light

If God is spirit, as children of God, we are spirit. We reflect God's essence through our inherent qualities. Furthermore, God is light and the source of all light energy. (1 John 1:5; James 1:17) As descendants of light and inhabitants of the earth, we are the light of the world. (Matthew 5:14)

The Spirit, God is the collective whole of consciousness over all things. You are spirit, a part of consciousness over the individual system you have been assigned. Your physical form is the object to express the moves of your spirit. Spirits move things by causing them to react. As your spirit engages with others, mutual reactions are inevitable. As the primary spirit responsible for the moves of your system, your fundamental purpose is to decide which sources will power the moves of your mind and body by selecting the nutrients and spirits to be absorbed as your energy.

The divine design is perfect. Transformation isn't to change who or what you are. It's a decision to increase the capacity of your spirit by filling it with higher quality energy to power the will of your moves towards the intentions of your heart's desires. Different energy qualities provide different types of reactions. Our entire experience is directly related to the light of our life.

> *"Then Jesus spoke to them again, saying, "I am the light of the world. He who follows Me shall not walk in darkness, but have the light of life." (John 8:12 NKJV)*

Heavenly Power of Cosmic Light

To effectively use your power, you must understand your light. Something magical happens when you desire to follow the highest light of the world and begin tuning into this power on a regular basis. You relearn how to communicate using the native language of light. As the frequency of your vibrational signal is moved closer to the highest power, you start to intuitively sense the energy shifts within you as a response from the targeted source of light. Then you're eventually led to the conceiver of all light.

> *Jesus said to him, "I am the way, the truth, and the*
> *life. No one comes to the Father except through Me."*
> *(John 14:6 NKJV)*

The intensity of your commitment to connect determines your signal strength. Once connected, you'll gradually start to understand the light within you and everything else in the universe. Information about existence is communicated through a wireless signal that reveals the interlinks of invisible light energy to visible light sources (all things). As you seek to reach the highest levels of awareness, the wisdom to obtain all else is also revealed.

> *"For nothing is secret that will not be revealed, nor*
> *anything hidden that will not be known and come to*
> *light." (Luke 8:17 NKJV)*

"Let there be light," was the first command spoken by God in the Bible. Sound is a form of energy caused by vibration (moving things). A voice as powerful as God's probably had a bang to it. **The vibration of God's first command is responsible for all motion, as the initial action of all reactions pertaining to light.** Vibrations are at the root of all things, including light. Movement causes heat. Heat causes faster movement, creating an ongoing energy cycle. And intense heat causes visible light.

The power of God conceives all things deriving from light. The light of God in all things is God's child. **God's firstborn and only creations are sources of light made to reflect His light** (although other elements may have preexisted light formation). There is only one light with endless possibilities expressed through unlimited forms of matter. All matter (excluding dark matter) is a source that absorbs and emits light as energy.

Spirits are invisible light energy waves emitted by light sources (everything). You absorb light energy from the environment and release it back into the surroundings. Electrical impulses can be considered as spirits moving through you, altering energy flow and triggering your reactions.

The power in the heavens above is cosmic light. Cosmic light sources are the primary emitters of radiation. Light energy is also radiation. Energy is the ability to move and cause other things to move.

If we are God's children and the light of the world, God's sun is heavenly light. The sun is the cause of all movement on Earth, including the chemical reactions of our bodies, allowing us to experience life. **The sun's spirit is a messenger with the attributes of an energy restorer (healer), force of life, heat, and the highest power over all earthly things.**

> *"And God made two great lights; the greater light to rule the day, and the lesser light to rule the night: he made the stars also. And God set them in the firmament of the heaven to give light upon the earth ..." (Genesis 1:16-17 KJV)*

We don't light ourselves. To speak of your energy and being the light, you can't disregard God's sun which gives you the light of life. All things on Earth reflect a degree of sunlight. Everything that doesn't produce its own visible glow can only be seen when it's lit by visible light.

A spiritual sense may be required to interpret spiritual truth, but there are nonspiritual alternatives to understanding the concept. Learning about the qualities of light energy (electromagnetic radiation) emitted from all sources of matter can shed light on comprehending the union of the seen and unseen. The characteristics of the things that are seen reflect the quality of the invisible powering spirit. Even if you cannot see the source, you can determine the type of light based on observing the reflection.

Everything is illuminated according to its relative position to the light. Your ability to see things clearly and reflect the light subsides as you move away from the light source. This also applies to your mental ability to think with clarity and positivity. When you are aligned with the highest power directly overhead, you reflect the most radiance and see this light reflected in everything else within range. On a sunny day your mood is more energized and everything appears vibrant.

The world is never in complete darkness due to the heavenly power of cosmic light. To see signs of light in the darkest hours, you must distance yourself from artificial light sources and readjust your focus. Your experience is linked to your exposure to light. A lack of energy or anything else is a lack of life-giving light in that area. You must see your conditions under the perspective of a brighter light. The nighttime sky shows light and darkness as part of the same field, but they are distinctly differentiated by their qualities. Therefore, both are parts of life. Remain consciously connected to the highest power to shine like a star.

> *"And take heed, lest you lift your eyes to heaven, and when you see the sun, the moon, and the stars, all the host of heaven, you feel driven to worship them and serve them, which the Lord your God has given to all the peoples under the whole heaven as a heritage."* (Deuteronomy 4:19 NKJV)

Surrounded by Spirits

> *"By faith we understand that the worlds were framed by the word of God, so that the things which are seen were not made of things which are visible."* (Hebrew 11:3 NKJV)

God's word is the vibration of light energy which makes things move. **Energy is part of everything, yet it is invisible to the human eye.** It is the primordial substance of existence. The sun and all derivative light sources emit invisible light energy. In addition to heat or a degree of reflected light, the light waves also transport information. **Spirit is invisible light energy that alters the perception of physical senses and the perspective of the mind.** The spirit (light) has a range of energy qualities that trigger chemical reactions within your body. These reactions can be sensed physically, emotionally, or mentally.

The stimuli of physical senses are rarely tuned out enough to notice the superpower of the spirits providing all objects the ability to be what they are. The physical and spiritual layers exist as inseparable parts of a single creation. To tune into spiritual signals, you must redirect your focus to the powering force within all.

Everything Is a Source of Light

Everything is a source of light with an invisible component or spirit. Only a tiny portion of the full light spectrum is visible light to humans. We don't see the spirits traveling through space or the electrical currents that flow through us and throughout other forms of matter.

Visible light is produced by incandescent, luminescent, or illuminated matter. Our sun and stars are forms of matter that light themselves and emit visible light as an incandescent source caused by intense heat. Objects emitting heat at a temperature above 525 °C become visible, producing a glow. **Heat is a sign of the rapid random movement of atoms and molecules (kinetic energy) within a substance.**

Luminescence is caused by absorbing energy from the sun, then releasing the excess as visible light.

You can see incandescent or luminescent sources that create their own visible light but not the light energy traveling *from* them through space. Signs of light traveling through space are made visible by reflecting off particles or objects, such as the moon and other forms of matter. Objects that don't light themselves are considered secondary light sources. This includes our planet and most earthly things.

Lit by Light

> *"For You will light my lamp; The Lord my God will enlighten my darkness." (Psalm 18:28 NKJV)*

We are lit by the primary sources of cosmic light and the secondary worldly sources derived from them. Your reactions reflect your light sources. Most matter is a secondary light source. It's illuminated or visible by being lit or reflecting light from another source. Cosmic light energy interacts with the particles of Earth, making visibility possible. However, above Earth's atmosphere, space appears dark and cold with the sun as a distant ball of white light, yet Earth is well-lit as it reflects this light.

The invisible electrical component pervading matter interlinks all light sources, with God's sun being the most prominent source for Earth. The interaction of spirits (invisible light energy) from everything in existence is the catalyst for continuous reactions throughout the universe. All matter emits light energy or radiation just like the sun, but most objects aren't hot enough to produce visible light, though some are luminescent. Therefore, all matter emits a spirit and radiates heat (temperatures above absolute zero).

The electrical current within matter creates an energy field around the subject. In spiritual terms, this field is the soul that contains the light of the body. It's often depicted in religious art by a crown of light rays, a sun, a halo, or a nimbus surrounding the head of an enlightened or sacred figure.

Messengers of Light

"Now we have received not the spirit of the world, but the Spirit who is from God, that we might understand

the things freely given to us by God. And we impart
this in words not taught by human wisdom but taught
by the Spirit, interpreting spiritual truths to those
who are spiritual." (1 Corinthians 2:12-13)

Existence is a message, and all light sources are messengers reflecting signs of light. And **the messiah is the light within you.**

All objects are signs of energy, and your emitted spirits are traveling energy waves that carry messages. Within the massive communication system of the universe, information is conveyed as two types of signals. The brain processes both physical and energy signals as electrical impulses, which trigger chemical reactions that form our sensations. Essentially, all detected signals are moving parts that cause further movement.

Communication systems work by connecting the energy signals of two or more sources. Everything is a source for energy to work through. Energy sources constantly convey a message. In turn, all signals convey a message regarding the energy quality working through the object that transmits the signal.

The quality of your inner light reflects your message to the world. Your life conveys a different message to each observer. We are all witnessing, interpreting, and reacting to the effects of light within us and around us from different perspectives. Any spiritual or physical interaction with your energy field or body will either brighten or dim your light relative to your position to being restored by the highest power.

Existence isn't a mystery if you look toward the light. Signs of light can be perceived from anything within range to be sensed mentally or physically.

> *"For since the creation of the world, His invisible* attributes *are clearly seen, being understood by the things that are made,* even *His eternal power and Godhead, so that they are without excuse ..."* *(Romans 1:20 NKJV)*

Linked to Light

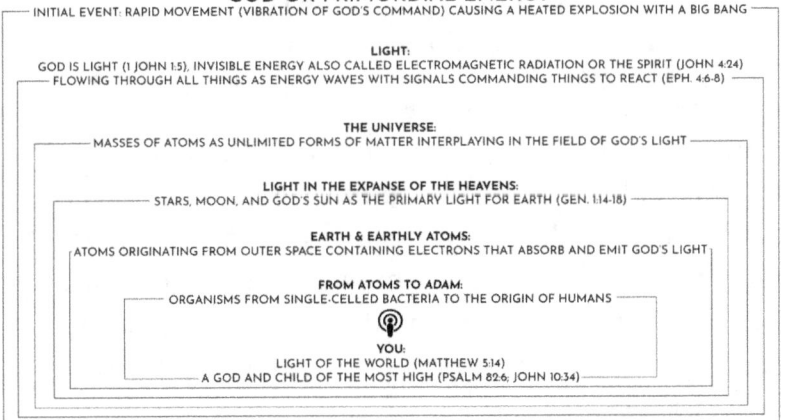

THE VISIBLE AND INVISIBLE LINEAGE OF ALL THINGS EVOLVING FROM THE SOURCE OF LIGHT

FATHER OF ALL LIGHTS (JAMES 1:17):

GOD OR PRIMORDIAL ENERGY

INITIAL EVENT: RAPID MOVEMENT (VIBRATION OF GOD'S COMMAND) CAUSING A HEATED EXPLOSION WITH A BIG BANG

LIGHT:
GOD IS LIGHT (1 JOHN 1:5), INVISIBLE ENERGY ALSO CALLED ELECTROMAGNETIC RADIATION OR THE SPIRIT (JOHN 4:24) FLOWING THROUGH ALL THINGS AS ENERGY WAVES WITH SIGNALS COMMANDING THINGS TO REACT (EPH. 4:6-8)

THE UNIVERSE:
MASSES OF ATOMS AS UNLIMITED FORMS OF MATTER INTERPLAYING IN THE FIELD OF GOD'S LIGHT

LIGHT IN THE EXPANSE OF THE HEAVENS:
STARS, MOON, AND GOD'S SUN AS THE PRIMARY LIGHT FOR EARTH (GEN. 1:14-18)

EARTH & EARTHLY ATOMS:
ATOMS ORIGINATING FROM OUTER SPACE CONTAINING ELECTRONS THAT ABSORB AND EMIT GOD'S LIGHT

FROM ATOMS TO ADAM:
ORGANISMS FROM SINGLE-CELLED BACTERIA TO THE ORIGIN OF HUMANS

YOU:
LIGHT OF THE WORLD (MATTHEW 5:14)
A GOD AND CHILD OF THE MOST HIGH (PSALM 82:6; JOHN 10:34)

The genetic information from your ancestors is contained within your physical form, but your energy derives itself from cosmic light. You're not only linked to the light, but you're also connected to the creator of light.

"At that day you will know that I am in My Father, and you in Me, and I in you." (John 14:20 NKJV)

Atoms are the basic units of all things. Within atoms are electrons that absorb the energy of photons, which are particles of light. This energy is processed while causing moves throughout your body and then released from your body. We are all linked to the light emitted by everything within the environment, and our connection to the sun is our link to larger cosmic systems. The sun's heliosphere is linked to the galactic cosmic rays of the Milky Way, and the Milky Way is linked to other galaxies which collectively fill the universe within the Spirit of God.

Your physical body is bound to earth, but the power source of your being expands across the entire cosmos. Mental and physical trips expand consciousness. However, physical destinations aren't portals to reach the required energy capacity of your divine destiny. The portal is within us. By using the tool of imagination, you can see yourself where you want to be before you physically arrive.

Nothing travels faster than the speed of light. Your thoughts travel at this speed. You aren't designed by nature to travel through outer space in a physical body. You are equipped with a light body to surpass physical restraints while the body remains grounded. In other words, don't send your body to a battle designed to be fought with spiritual strength. The mind rises and shines while the body is meant to explore and experience life on Earth.

The light you emit can travel anywhere within the universal field. By navigating your attention to the energy of the creator, you can overcome the world. Bypassing worldly distractions that hinder growth will eventually lead to where all lanes merge into one with Light.

"You are of God, little children, and have overcome them, because He who is in you is greater than he who is in the world." (1 John 4:4 NKJV)

KEY POINTS | LIGHT OF THE WORLD

- The sun's spirit is a messenger with the attributes of an energy restorer (healer), force of life, heat, and the highest power of all earthly things.

- Identifying as a spiritual being sparks curiosity to learn more about the inherited traits of your light and how to effectively use them.

- The family tree of your light lineage links the power of the creator and cosmic light to your light.

- Heavenly power is cosmic light. The light of the world includes all things inhabiting the world.

- Light energy is the invisible core of your being. We absorb, use, and emit invisible light energy (radiation).

- Spirit is invisible light energy that alters the perception of physical senses and the perspective of the mind. It is the emitted characteristics of a light source.

- Life is a chain reaction caused by vibrations that create light.

- Movement causes heat, which is a type of light energy. Intense heat causes visible light. There wouldn't be visible light without rapid movement to generate heat.

- The intensity of your light is significantly less than the sun, but your spirit is still influential enough to cause electrical impulses within others.

Spiritual Spark Exercise

God created light, and you inherit its power. However, it's impossible to reflect light that isn't within your range. To constantly reflect the energy of a particular spirit, you must constantly be within the range of this light.

Mentally visualize you are outside in the sunlight. Then walk inside your home and into a dark closet without windows. Are you still visibly reflecting the sunlight? Your relative position to the light source is key. Even though you may no longer be reflecting the light you were exposed to, your mind and body might still be reacting from the last interaction, eventually requiring restoration to remain under its influence.

As inhabitants of Earth, we turn away from God's sun, not the other way around. However, rotation and cycles are natural conditions of life on Earth. The sun is always shining as the highest source of light, but it can only be seen and reflected off objects within its range.

We don't always have to be within physical range since we have a spiritual component. You can mentally focus your attention to any source to establish a connection. In return, your thoughts are infused by the subject and expressed through your emotions and behavior.

Think how the qualities of different light sources change the way you and your surroundings appear. The color, intensity, and position of the light can make things appear from dark to light with subsequent reactions that can cause you to feel drained or energized. Reflect on the light you radiate into the world and your sources of influence. Take note of the spirits emitted by other people or things that uplift your spirits. The quality of this light gives life.

CHAPTER 3

YOUR INHERITANCE AS LIGHT

"Wisdom is good with an inheritance: and by it there is profit to them that see the sun"
(Ecclesiastes 7:11 KJV).

The Healing Spirit of God's Sun

Disregarding the most powerful light within physical range devalues its power to move through you and make changes in your life. **The inheritance from sunlight is life's energy and its range of qualities.** Energy healing benefits are valuable entitlements, and light energy is the power altering perspective, perception, and bodily functions. What's more, the spirit of God's sun is the invisible light that travels through space, through us, and is reflected by all things we interact with on Earth.

Products protecting us from potential sunlight damage are promoted more than the sun's *free* life-sustaining energy. Electricity is an amazing tool when used properly. However, a lack of understanding about its power could lead to misuse with harmful or deadly consequences. This is the nature of all light sources, including us.

Sunlight isn't some life-threatening force that we should fear. Nor should we apply potential toxins as a protective layer between ourselves and the primary source of light. In many cases, it's the ingredients in the products we use daily that weaken our tolerance of ultra-violet (UV) light.

Our body produces a natural sunscreen. Melanin production is a defense reaction to UV rays. It's not a cosmetic enhancement to change our skin tone to a desired shade. Artificial sunscreens are designed for overexposure to sunlight or sensitive skin. There are appropriate times of day and durations for sun gazing and sunbathing. In most cases, if we know how to properly use the light for its intended purpose, we won't attempt to block direct access, other than glare protection for sight.

Warmth from the sun can be tremendously soothing to the skin and relaxing for the mind. In addition, sun gazing at the appropriate time has numerous benefits. However, we must realize all attributes have opposites set by the laws of nature. Excessive heat burns and evaporates the water content in our body which causes internal issues. In addition, overexposing the eyes to bright light can impair vision. Knowing the characteristics of the most powerful light and applying the knowledge is our first layer of protection for our health.

The emitted light we sense from the sun is invisible infrared (IR) or thermal radiation as heat and visible light processed as sight. Our skin and eyes interact with the sun's invisible IR and UV rays. Visible light is the only portion we can see. We experience the effects of UV radiation as a sunburn or tanning sensation on the skin, but the beneficial biological implications are processed as electrical signals with internal chemical reactions.

An uplifted spirit, increased energy, and relaxation are a few inherited qualities from the sun. Sunlight stimulates the pleasant effects of serotonin production—95% of which is produced in the intestines. So, exposure to sunlight can indirectly influence the activity of gut microbiome (bacteria) by impacting serotonin levels. The bacteria interact with the brain through the gut-brain axis. Therefore, **sunlight exposure and the food we ingest are linked to our brain health.**

"Serotonin plays a key role in such body functions as mood, sleep, digestion, nausea, wound healing, bone health, blood clotting, and sexual desire."[1] Because of its positive impact, bright light mimicking daylight is used to treat various diseases as a form of therapy. The commonly used terms for this type of treatment are light therapy, phototherapy, and heliotherapy. Seasonal affective disorder (SAD) (a type of depression caused by the lack of exposure to daylight) can also be treated with light boxes designed to deliver a therapeutic dose of bright light.

Meet the Rays

The three main types of UV light rays are UVA, UVB, and UVC. Sun gazing is recommended when the UV intensity is at its lowest, which is just after sunrise and right before sunset. UVA light penetrates the skin at deeper levels than UVB and can contribute to premature skin aging and the risk of cancer if overexposed. UVB triggers Vitamin D production and is the healthiest UV ray. UVC light is harmful to humans, but used as a sanitizer, it is effective for killing bacteria and viruses.

Photosynthesis is the process of converting light energy into chemical energy. This process isn't limited to plants. Our entire experience is based on the spirit providing us the ability to react. While other nutrients are obtained from our food, vitamin D is a micronutrient synthesized in the skin through a photosynthetic reaction triggered by exposure to UVB radiation. UV touches the brain and central neuroendocrine system to reset the body's self-regulating process that allows organisms to maintain stability, including reproduction, growth, metabolism and energy balance, and stress responsiveness.[2] "This invites multiple therapeutic applications of UV radiation, for example, in the management of autoimmune and mood disorders, addiction, and obesity."[2]

Like plants, our survival is significantly dependent on the reactions caused by our interactions with air (oxygen),

water, sunlight and Earth's surface. Without sunlight, our health would deteriorate significantly due to vitamin D deficiency and other light inducing chemical reactions.

Syncing with the Sun

"For the Lord God is a sun and shield: the Lord will give grace and glory: no good thing will he withhold from them that walk uprightly." (Psalm 84:11 KJV)

Light has significant effects beyond our vision. **God created the light (from which we derived) and synchronized our bodies to react to light energy.** We are solar-powered beings with Earth's surface as our grounding station. Earth and sunlight have properties that naturally heal and balance your energy.

The heat from the sun drives Earth's climate system, and the gravitational pull of the moon controls the tides of the oceans. It doesn't take rocket science to realize we are also strongly affected by the objects of the cosmos. For regulating bodily functions and balancing the energy of your system, the sun is your primary source of energy, in addition to nutrients from food.

Circadian rhythms are the body's natural twenty-four-hour cycle of physical, mental, and behavioral changes. The circadian clock is associated with the inter-organ communications of the body. These rhythms are primarily influenced by light and darkness. (The natural blue light during the day is also a factor.) Some of the functions affected by these rhythms also have behavioral fluctuations associated with sleep-wake and feeding-fasting cycles, while others are solely dependent on time-of-day.[3]

Various components of the endocrine system exhibit time-of-day-dependent rhythms that affect the governing mechanisms of cellular hormone action.[3] "The endocrine system, made up of all the body's different hormones, regulates all biological processes in the body from conception through adulthood and into old age, including the development of the brain and nervous system, the growth and function of the reproductive system, as well as the metabolism and blood sugar levels."[4]

Serotonin converts to melatonin—both of which are affected by exposure to daylight. Melatonin is a hormone that helps regulate the sleep-wake cycle. It is suppressed in the presence of blue light. In the absence of daylight, when exposed to darkness, melatonin is released. Due to the high-energy stimulation of blue, artificial blue light can be harmful when there is excess exposure after sunset and before sunrise because it can disrupt the natural sleep cycle.

Dim light should be used between sunset and sunrise. Your body is synched to the cycle of natural sunlight. The initial exposure to bright light in the morning should come from the rising of the sun—even if you wake before sunrise. If sunlight is inaccessible at sunrise, artificial bright light can be an alternative.

Abnormal circadian rhythms may be linked to several health conditions. Your interactions with UVB and blue light have effects associated with behavior, sleep, sex, weight gain (fat cells), metabolism, appetite, ability to block pain, energy, mood, stress, alertness, skin pigmentation, and antimicrobial and anti-inflammatory functions.

The protection you need isn't to block the sun, unless you're faced with conditions requiring overexposure or experience sensitivity. The greater concern is underexposure to natural daylight and overexposure to artificial blue light. Keep in mind that UVB light is absorbed best with bare skin exposure.

The time we go to sleep and wake up isn't as crucial. There are a ton of products available to minimize blue light toxicity from the use of electronic devices and bulbs. Most devices have nighttime features. There are UV light therapy lamps available for situations causing insufficient exposure to daylight. And man-made grounding products are also available to enhance your energy-regulating practices.

"The Lord is your keeper; The Lord is your shade at your right hand. The sun shall not strike you by day, Nor the moon by night." (Psalms 121:5-6 NKJV)

KEY POINTS | INHERITING LIGHT

- God created light sources capable of emitting life-sustaining energy, but they can have the opposite effect if misused, which also applies to humans.

- Sunlight is the most intense light with the greatest impact on all systems within the solar system.

- Sunlight is the force of all life on Earth and the primary energy restorer of all things.

- Sunlight is a no-cost therapeutic healing energy that interacts with the brain and central neuroendocrine system to reset body homeostasis.

- Sunlight acts as a master energy switch for triggering the chemical reactions within humans that help regulate mood, sleep, appetite, digestion, memory, learning, body temperature, and sexual behavior.

- The internal clock within each cell of our body is synched to sunlight as the circadian rhythm.

- Vitamin D is an essential micronutrient that is a direct result of a photosynthetic reaction caused by UVB.

- Spirits are uplifted by UV light, triggering the release of serotonin, the happy hormone.

- Body pain is minimized as UV light reduces pain perception by the release of endorphins.

- Sunset stimulates rest for the body, mind, and spirit by regulating melatonin production, which helps regulate sleep patterns.

- Stress is reduced by exposure to sunlight, which stimulates the release of peptides to counteract the effects of stress hormones.

- UV light triggers a shield of protection against harmful exposure through the production of melanin.

- As part-energy beings, we have inherited the qualities of generating heat and being the receiver and emitter of spiritual energy that can alter consciousness.

- Lack of sunlight can contribute to several health issues.

Spiritual Spark Exercise

Take a minute to acknowledge the power of the sun. Go outside to get direct exposure or recall a previous experience. Write (or mentally note) how the sunlight affects your body and mind. Give thanks for its warmth, radiant light, mood-boosting properties, and life-sustaining energy.

CHAPTER 4

THE DECLINING HEALTH OF DRAINED SPIRITS

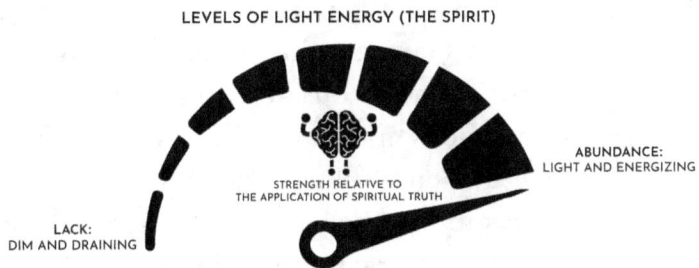

LEVELS OF LIGHT ENERGY (THE SPIRIT)

STRENGTH RELATIVE TO
THE APPLICATION OF SPIRITUAL TRUTH

ABUNDANCE:
LIGHT AND ENERGIZING

LACK:
DIM AND DRAINING

Healing Along the Path of Ascension

Gaining strength to elevate your position is done by frequently renewing your light. You are designed to be depleted and restored by the spirits within the environment. Your source of power and applied knowledge of how to maintain your light determine your state of health.

The earth and the sun are the largest sources of energy within our range. Everything on Earth is a source that emits radiation, but the sun is the only consistent light. It's not affected by the conditions within Earth's atmosphere, and most importantly, it's outside of man's control.

Preservation of your health and the environment should be a top priority. Without good health, it's difficult to focus on anything else. As organisms, we are designed to perform best when our internal and external systems are organized structures. Performing best is difficult to do in a world of chaos. **Misalignment of your energy system in relation to restorative power is an issue preventing you from gaining the strength to manifest the conditions you desire.** Throughout your journey, you are rising from unhealthy habits, situations, thoughts, and emotions that can manifest as disease or mental blocks. As you are being uplifted, you can aspire to support the journey of others, which can consequently continue to raise your spirit.

Self-inflicted Pain and Suffering

Life is a series of decisions that lead to experiences with a positive, neutral, or negative effect on your well-being. The decisions you make have the power to change your life's course. **The option with the most potential to elevate your current state by positive means is likely the most beneficial decision in the grand scheme of things.**

Have we collectively become so distracted that progressing toward a higher state of consciousness or uplifting our spirit is a declining interest of humankind? Is this lack of interest creating an identity crisis, causing the behavior of our self-inflicted pain and suffering?

Are we accepting the manipulations of the mind that lead to poor decision-making concerning our overall well-being? Are we willingly adopting the conditions that contribute to prolonged stress, chronic disease, and mental illness, rather than preventing them or treating the root cause to eradicate them? Have these health issues become part of the normal standards for living?

The Rise of Declining Health

We are all vulnerable to the onset of disease. According to a publication issued by the Centers for Disease Control and Prevention in 2024, "An increasing proportion of people in America are dealing with multiple chronic conditions; 42% have 2 or more, and 12% have at least 5."[5] Declining health is an issue the entire world is facing.

Needless to say, the healthcare industry is an extremely lucrative business with increasing profit projections for many years to come. Despite the economic benefits for those employed or financially invested in industries linked to the healthcare system, money isn't more valuable than life or the quality of life.

You are your primary care provider, not the professional you may see periodically. We can't expect a drastic change to be made from an institutional level to address personalized care. This is a matter we should take seriously for ourselves.

Implementing a daily regimen involving preventive measures could reduce health risks. We could make lifestyle changes to remove the unsupportive conditions of good health. This tactic is more effective than ongoing treatments of an identified illness while under the same circumstances that caused the issue.

There are many contributing factors to your health, some of which are outside of your control. Lifestyle is a hefty contributor. **Quality of life includes your physical and light energy aspects.** Maintaining your well-being involves more than incorporating the proper nutrients and physical activity. The continuous flow of absorbed light energy alters your electrical current. It's not to be taken lightly.

It is your responsibility to optimize your health and the conditions for restoration. However, a major lifestyle adjustment can be challenging for most people. The prerequisite is a mindset shift to power consciousness with a new perspective that will inspire you to make the necessary changes.

> *"And do not be conformed to this world, but be transformed by the renewing of your mind, that you may prove what is that good and acceptable and perfect will of God." (Romans 12:2 NKJV)*

Health Is Harmony

We are familiar with the aspects of ourselves that we can perceive with the physical senses. However, some of us lack the basic knowledge of the mechanisms beneath the skin layer and how they operate. In addition, the role of the soul is almost completely ignored. Energy healing is viewed as esoteric, but we are constantly reflecting, absorbing, emitting, and reacting to spiritual light energy. We don't see stress moving toward us or exiting the body, but we can experience the effect.

> "For what profit is it to a man if he gains the whole world, and loses his own soul? Or what will a man give in exchange for his soul?" (Matthew 16:26 NKJV).

The individual parts of your structure work together for the survival of the whole. For your well-being, your body, soul, and spirit must be powered by a restorative source. Even the planets of the solar system keep orbit around the sun. The most powerful light has the capacity to make you shine; however, it's most effective when you are within close range.

> "... May every part of you be set apart for God. May your spirit and your soul and your body be kept complete ..." (1 Thessalonians 5:23 NLV).

The spirit is the driving force of life but is often treated as a backseat passenger. **Your invisible energy current is**

diligently at work regardless of being noticed. However, with an awareness of consciousness, you can provide your system with the proper care. There is an immense focus on physical fitness, entertainment, beauty regimens, and making money, while spiritual practices or mental health are often overlooked. Energy healing is an emerging practice but still widely disregarded as a serious treatment option.

Full Stomach, Drained Spirits

We often use the terms "vibe" or "energy" to describe moods. How much consideration do we give to our spirit beyond the casual description of how we feel? The spirit fills the soul, which affects your ability to perform.

Most people who have access to three meals a day may rarely opt to skip a meal. **How many times a day do you break to refill your soul?** Sunlight and Earth's surface are natural energy neutralizers for the mind and body, but you must make the connection. A soul with a drained spirit is energy-deprived, even if the associated physical body has a full stomach.

The primary benefit of food isn't to strengthen consciousness. Food provides the energy for the body to function, grow, and maintain body mass. Spirits provide the willpower for consciousness forming the perspective for desires, intentions, thoughts, emotions, and behavioral acts. Consider high-quality foods that have adequate nutrients. They can protect the body against unwanted growth such as excess weight, cancer cells, and tumors. Engaging in high-spirited interactions can protect against forming harmful thoughts or emotions which can lead to unhealthy acts.

> *"'Man shall not live by bread alone, but by every word that proceeds from the mouth of God.'"(Matthew 4:4 NKJV)*

Your quality of life is linked to the qualities of the foods you intake and the light energy (spirits) you absorb. The quality of anything stems from its source and how it's maintained. Someone with a full stomach can still be malnourished from a lack of adequate nutrition. Malnutrition can be presented as undernutrition, overweight, and micronutrient deficiencies. Overeating has no benefits. Unused energy is potential energy stored as fat. A surplus of nutrients is unnecessary unless you are planning on conditions with restrictive access to food. Otherwise, excess fat can negatively impact health.

Even the healthiest foods are subject to factors that warrant caution. There are natural substances in plants and nuts, such as anti-nutrients that can be difficult to digest, reducing the absorption rates of nutrients. This means that even if you are consuming the recommended nutrient levels, you may only be absorbing a fraction of the full amount. Other factors to caution are added substances to plant-based and animal products that include pesticides, antibiotics, or growth hormones.

QUALITY RANGE OF LIGHT ENERGY & CHEMICAL ENERGY

QUALITY RANGE OF LIGHT ENERGY (SPIRIT)

	WEAK MIND		STRONG MIND	
LACK AND	IGNORANCE		WISDOM	RESTORATIVE
LIMITATIONS	LOW LEVEL OF CONSCIOUSNESS		HIGH LEVEL OF CONSCIOUSNESS	ABUNDANT LIGHT

DRAINING -   + LIFE-GIVING

SEPARATION	LOW FREQUENCY		HIGH FREQUENCY	ONENESS
FROM LIGHT	WEAK SIGNAL		STRONG SIGNAL	WITH LIGHT

MORE INFLUENCED BY WORLDLY THINGS ← OR → MORE INSPIRED BY INNER STRENGTH

ABSORBED AND EMITTED ELECTROMAGNETIC RADIATION (LIGHT) OR SPIRITS
• INTERACTIONS WITH EVERYTHING IN THE UNIVERSE RECEIVED AS ELECTRICAL IMPULSES PROCESSED AS
SENSATIONS TRIGGERING REACTIONS THAT CAUSES YOU TO MOVE, CHANGE, AND TRANSFORM

SOUL | CONSCIOUSNESS
• ELECTROMAGNETIC FIELD (EMF) SURROUNDING THE BODY
• OUTER CONTAINER HOLDING OUR INDIVIDUAL SYSTEM (BODY, MIND, & SPIRIT) TOGETHER
• LIGHT ENERGY RELEASED AND ABSORBED RELATED TO CHEMICAL REACTIONS THAT ALTER ALL
MENTAL, EMOTIONAL, & PHYSICAL ACTIVITIES

PHYSICAL BODY
• PHYSICAL FORM CREATED BY AND REACTING TO THE COMMANDS OF LIGHT ENERGY
• A MASS OF CHARGED PARTICLES FOR SPIRITUAL ENERGY TO WORK THROUGH
• OBSERVING RECEIVER AND TRANSMITTER OF ENERGY SIGNALS

ABSORBED CHEMICAL ENERGY FROM FOOD AND OTHER SUBSTANCES
• PRIMARILY NECESSARY NUTRIENTS TO MAINTAIN THE PHYSICAL SUBSTANCE OF THE BODY
• ENERGY IS ABSORBED BY INHALATION, INGESTION, INJECTION, DERMAL (SKIN), EARS, AND EYES

QUALITY RANGE OF CHEMICAL ENERGY (NUTRIENTS)

UNHEALTHY	HEALTHY
DISEASE CONTRIBUTOR	EASILY DIGESTED
LOW-QUALITY	HIGH-QUALITY

DRAINING -   → + LIFE-GIVING

LOW VIBRATION	HIGH VIBRATION
INADEQUATE OR EXCESS	SUFFICIENT
PROCESSED OR PACKAGED FOODS	FRESH WHOLE FOODS

Micronutrients Are Major

While often downplayed, micronutrient deficiencies are serious threats to our health. A known deficiency can be an indicator that other micronutrient levels are also inadequate. "There are six major classes of nutrients essential for human health: carbohydrates, lipids, proteins, vitamins, minerals, and water."[6] The essential nutrients for complete protein contain nine amino acids.

There are approximately twenty-five different types of micronutrients the body needs. Most lab tests only focus on a handful at the request of a doctor when there are signs of a potential issue. Requesting a comprehensive metabolic panel (CMP) blood test without any symptoms is an option well worth the expense.

Protein provides the amino acids for cell repair, growth, and development. Carbohydrates are the primary source of energy for the body. It's meant to be used for the ability to do work, not stored. A small amount of essential fatty acids is required for the absorption of vitamin A, vitamin D, and vitamin E.

The recommended daily allowance (RDA) is a basis for the mass population. **Maintaining healthy energy levels should include personalized measures.** Once we reach a certain level of consciousness, the quality of our mental and physical health is a priority. Our diet and activities start to align with our level of consciousness as a reflection of our relation to the light. The more we identify with the light, the more we gravitate towards lighter foods that are easy to digest. The focus is more on sufficient quantities and quality of nutrients to perform the physical works of the Spirit. This may include more nourishment from nature.

> *"For he who eats and drinks in an unworthy manner eats and drinks judgment to himself, not discerning the Lord's body. For this reason many are weak and sick among you, and many sleep." (1 Corinthians 11:29-30 NKJV)*

The Endangered Superpower of Optimal Health

Having the necessary awareness to comprehend the connection between our light, other light sources on Earth, sunlight, and the creator of the light is the endangered superpower of optimal health. **The lineage of our light energy is important knowledge when considering our health.** The root of the universal family tree is light. It is a part of everything. Therefore, we're all relatives of light. However, this lineage is often disregarded when the focus is on our physical forms. Moreover, the sun is still the primary force responsible for maintaining all structures within its solar system.

We don't have the capability to perform beyond the capacity of our energy intake. A spiritual snack will not be sufficient energy for certain situations. We perform according to the qualities of our absorbed energy sources. Without sufficient energy, we won't have the mental, emotional, or physical strength for peak performance.

Countless scenarios can alter your energy levels. However, there are only two types of energy that are used for the ability to do work: spiritual (radiation or light energy) and nutritional (chemical energy). Being mentally and physically healthy is becoming extinct. If we are healthy, we are better equipped to handle the circumstances of life.

Health concerns can overwhelm the mind, causing you to become stuck in survival mode. It can be a difficult task to focus on uplifting your spirit in moments when you are being mentally or physically drained. However, it's possible if we've already attained a certain level of mental strength along with continued self-healing practices or have the support of others.

Healing is the process of restoring healthy levels of physical and spiritual energy. Whether it be mentally, emotionally, or physically, we are all in need of healing from something. There is no shame in participating in healing practices. It isn't admitting something is wrong, it's recognizing the maintenance requirements to function properly and taking action accordingly.

Your fight for survival begins the moment you are conceived. You are constantly using and replenishing the energy of your system. Healing is an ongoing cycle. Nature is cyclical.

KEY POINTS | THE DECLINING HEALTH OF DRAINED SPIRITS

- You must consider your whole self when addressing factors concerning your health. The spirit and physical body need replenishment throughout the day.

- Your physical and mental energy levels are decreased and increased by your participation in this world. A lifestyle conducive to energy restoration is essential to your performance and health.

- Elevating consciousness is also a journey towards a healthier lifestyle.

- Internal or external disorder causes stress-related health issues that are essentially the result of energy-draining conditions.

- The quality and quantity of your energy sources determine their replenishment ability. Excess or insufficient levels can be harmful.

- Everything can alter your energy, but your system is restored by only two types of energy: light energy (spiritual energy) and chemical energy (food).

- Your energy consumption should be relative to your energy usage. The recommended daily allowance (RDA) is a guide based on the estimated average requirement.

Spiritual Spark Exercise

Your health takes priority. Self-realization leads to energy healing for the mind, body, and emotions. Take a short break to stand in front of a mirror or sit with your eyes closed. Stack both hands over your heart with palms facing inward. If facing a mirror, look your reflection in the eyes (keep eyes closed if not) and give thanks to every cell in your body for working nonstop for your survival. Continue to express gratitude for your existence by considering the nutritional quality of your next meal and the quality of energy exchanges during future interactions.

Continue seeking energy sources that are conducive to higher energetic states of being. The input energy is relative to the output energy. To see a different perspective on life, you must consider the qualities of your energy sources.

Note your answers to the questions below:

- What commitment could you make to yourself starting now that would move you closer towards eating sufficient portions of high-quality nutrients?
- Who or what is the highest source of power elevating your mental energy or spirit and how often do you absorb the energy of this source?
- Is your power source providing the energy qualities needed to be the best version of yourself?

- Have you noticed the transformation in you and your surroundings that reflect the ideal life of your higher self?
- Is your life inspiring and energetic most of the time?
- On a scale of 1 to 10 or from weak to strong, how would you rate the intensity of your relationship to the force that created the universe? Now consider how to strengthen the connection.

CHAPTER 5

THE PURSUIT OF HIGHER CONSCIOUSNESS

Surpassing Mental Limitations

Our descension from heaven to Earth was more like a fall to the ground causing a temporary mental impairment. Forgetting who we are has weakened our conscious ability to connect to the source. We spend our lives gradually healing from the wounds of the human experience, while simultaneously rising in consciousness. As your mental strength increases, you awaken to the source of power within you. **As your level of consciousness continues to elevate, you start to recognize your poor judgment caused by your deluded perception of life.**

Once you have your health in check and basic survival needs met, it's an instinct to focus more on elevating consciousness to states of peace or enlightenment. Achieving higher states of consciousness is ascension toward the higher self. The process of embodying these traits is a simple concept but also a challenge for most people to accomplish. It takes strategic mindfulness to continuously sustain healthy energy levels.

You must surpass the mental limitations caused by the false information you have allowed to form your identity and perspective. Transforming self-perspective to sync with who you are by divine design is possible under the influence of spiritual truth. Transcending worldly conditions requires a conscious connection to a power source above earthly things. The most powerful energy with the ability to move things comes from the heavenly power of cosmic light.

The power of God's sun commands an entire solar system. The embedded power of your being is your link to this light and to the creator of light. Seeking sends an energy signal to your internal comforter, teacher, and guide to gradually uplift your mood and strengthen your mind. Your transformation is evidence of a spiritual vibration causing a chemical response within you. It is the reply from the Spirit to your silent vibrational call.

Renewing the Spirit of the Mind

We all have a mind, but the spirits we allow to influence it determines its strength. Regarding the human experience, a mind that is frequently directed to abundant power is the most powerful force in the universe. Consciousness is the foundation of existence. It's the faculty of all signals that move physical forms. A mind is like an empty vase to be filled with the spirit or light energy. High-spirited things radiate life-giving light. Renewing the spirit is restoring the energy of the mind with sources of light higher than your own. Weak minds become trapped, and strong minds become liberated.

The energy aspect of your interactions and the information capturing your attention interplay with your soul and physical body. The information you planted in your mind yesterday is directing your decisions for today. Changes aren't instant because the non-bearing trees need uprooting and new seeds must be cultivated to gain strength and provide beneficial energy. Simply wanting to change isn't enough for instant attainment of that change. It's a process.

Even with awareness, the pursuit of external things can take over your life causing you to become a busy doer. There are a ton of distractions that can overstimulate your physical senses. Attention traps leave little quality time, if any, to cultivate your true power. As a result, you may find yourself on auto-pilot, feeling stuck in a lifestyle that doesn't seem to reflect your true potential.

If we progressively work toward a desired mental state above all else, our outlook on life would look a lot different. All other desires would be easier to obtain with a stronger mind. A renewed mind may even replace the self-serving desires of the old mind with inspiration to contribute to this world, rather than wanting to gain something from it. Mental status is more valuable than anything gained by social status.

> *"... Put off your old self, which belongs to your former manner of life and is corrupt through deceitful desires, and to be renewed in the spirit of your minds, and to put on the new self, created after the likeness of God in true righteous and holiness." (Ephesians 4:22-24 ESV)*

Calibrating Mentality

Neglecting to develop your mind for a higher use is like being a bird that doesn't use its wings to fly. Instead, it walks the grounds, not realizing its potential to fly high with a bird's eye view of the world. **Could a different perspective empower us to make better decisions in alignment with optimal health, fulfilling roles, and authentic love for all?**

> *"Instead, we will speak the truth in love, growing in every way more and more like Christ, who is the head of his body, the church. He makes the whole body fit together perfectly. As each part does its own special work, it helps the other parts grow, so that the whole body is healthy and growing and full of love." (Ephesians 4:15-16 NLT)*

You must change your position to obtain a different perspective. Everything is a different version than it was a second ago, but subtle changes can go unnoticed. Over time, what will the quality of your spiritual light deposits and withdrawals amount to? The exact conditions of any moment will never be repeated. Change is always occurring; therefore, time is always passing.

Time is a measurement of changing moments. Be careful not to confuse elapsed time or the movement of things around you with your progression. The moves you make should be relevant to your personal growth. By changing the integrity of your inner self, your moves penetrate to deeper levels of your being.

Your external moves mimic internal strength. Making moves to merely adapt to the changes of your environment can still produce growth but at the minimal rate of a standard economic pay raise, which doesn't take personal performance into account.

Your moves should be calibrated to your intended purpose. It may be time to turn around, look in a new direction, or relocate. Each way would provide new scenery based on your moves. However, remaining at the same level may only produce a minor change. A higher altitude can eliminate low-level obstructions, which may appear as threats to your survival or distracting focal points.

Starting from where you are and rising above the obstacles of the world can aid in determining your next best move. Therefore, start by elevating your mind, not by moving external things. When you are uplifted, you have greater clarity to move in either direction with less effort. At this level, you realize you are no longer walking but are soaring by the force of your inner strength with high-spirited things surrounding you. Like a bird, you must learn to use your wings. This knowledge is taught by inner wisdom in the pursuit of a higher consciousness.

KEYNOTES | THE PURSUIT OF HIGHER CONSCIOUSNESS

Knowledge of your light isn't a ticket into a magical realm. Gaining the use of this power is a process. It's readily available at any time, but you must continue to surpass the current limitations of your mind. Embracing the characteristics of your authentic identity is done by positioning yourself closer to sources of light with the ability to transcend your mind. Light reveals truth. To triumph over delusional viewpoints, a portion of your attention must be dedicated to retrieving truth regularly. Pursuing a higher state of consciousness requires activating your link to higher power.

Spiritual Spark Exercise

Create a sacred space in your mind, dedicate a small area of your home, and add a recurring appointment on your calendar for cultivating your light. You can start with only a few minutes each day. Mark the event on your primary calendar as a high-priority event. Meeting with the highest power for restoration should be the highlight of your day. Personalize the experience with things that instantly uplift your spirits. Decorate your space with positive quotes that become mental notes. You could wear a piece of jewelry throughout the day that reminds you of your light. Make this occasion a full-blown ritual with your favorite beverage, meditation pillow or chair, audio tunes, essential oils, healing stones, a dedicated journal, throw cover, related books, or any other items to help you dive into your inner world with ease. This is your uninterrupted sacred moment to simply be.

CHAPTER 6

ASCENSION AS THE HIGHER SELF

"The sun also rises, and the sun goes down, And hastens to the place where it arose." (Ecclesiastes 1:5 NKJV)

Spiritual Rebirth

Descension to Earth is an opportunity to rise. Life is filled with moments designed for us to rise above our current level of consciousness and improve our physical conditions. Your habits of recharging will temporarily uplift your mind or take root to transform your mind. The impact of the effect is determined by the capacity of your powering sources and how often you are within range to absorb the light.

Higher quality spiritual energy is a force to be consciously activated and utilized as a superpower. Your higher self is the version of you embodied by a higher spirit. Your highest self is you, spiritually transformed, renewed, and set apart for God's purpose—also known as spiritual rebirth, which is a departure from any part of life that separates you from God. Physical death is not a requirement. Rather, the aspects of yourself that separate you from expressing the light of limitless power must die. When you are no longer bound by physical restraints, your mind is free to ascend under the influence of its powering source. Realizing you are one with this power.

> "God is Spirit, and those who worship Him must worship in spirit and truth." (John 4:24 NKJV)

The Spirit of God, or the creator, is the highest force and greatest source of information. The Spirit is the invisible light energy of all things within the cosmic field. To accept God is to accept all things created by God. There is no separation. The same goes for self-acceptance. Both the positive and negative conditions contribute to your life.

Self-reinvention by the conception of rebirth is detaching from the false identity traits we've accepted as true. There is nothing to become because you already are, always have been, and forever will be who you are meant to be in each moment of your life. Rather than reinventing or becoming, you are embracing your authentic identification as your awareness increases. You gradually transition into intentional living as a positive light for yourself and others.

Power of Association

"He who does not love does not know God, for God is love" (1 John 4:8 NKJV).

Your light is associated with the light that formed the universe. It has the power to create and move things. God is love. Love is the Spirit of your life. The most powerful act of love is creating life-giving light. As God's children, we can choose to radiate loving light by demonstrating actions that support life. We are formed by, sustained with, and emitters of love's power. Although, how we use the power is our decision.

The invisible energy signals of the spirits you associate with alter your mind and move through your body. Your spirit also has this effect on others. "Death and life are in the power of the tongue ..." (Proverbs 18:21) but the messages of spiritual energy are silent.

You must be aware of the implications of invisible spirits emitted by things. You may have partial control over what you expose your mind and body to, but you don't control your system's reactions to the things you absorb. The impact of spiritual signals is highly subjective to the quality of the emitting and receiving spirits. It's best not to drive on empty.

"It is the Spirit who gives life; the flesh profits nothing. The words that I speak to you are spirit, and they are life." (John 6:63 NKJV)

One Truth with Countless Interpretations

Some people demonstrate they are more religious than godly. A belief in God, an association with organized religion, or identifying as a spiritual person is not required to ascend to a higher consciousness. A belief in a force greater than your own and tuning into this source regularly is a requirement. An open-minded individual may have the ability to benefit from truth presented by numerous resources. **Other people's versions of spiritual truth should only be viewed as sparks towards gaining your own interpretation.**

Organized religion is a man-made, structured system. While the term "religion" is defined as the belief in and worship of a superhuman power or powers (especially a God or gods), the associated practices could be personal or institutional. You could be considered religious even as the only member of your own religion. The term "spiritual" can be rephrased as an awareness and understanding of our energy aspects.

> *"… one God and Father of all, who is above all, and through all, and in you all." (Ephesians 4:6 NKJV)*

We can't see the totality of God because we're within God and God is within us. We are within God's energy body, and this energy flows through our physical body sustaining life. We witness parts of God as everything created and God's spirit as the energy providing the ability for all movement creating moments.

Strengthening the mind can be achieved by focusing on information and participating in activities that empower the perspective of your thoughts. The attributes of absorbed spirits work through your system and reflect the character of the sources that emitted the spirits you have embodied. An authentic connection to the Spirit of God is evident by the moves of how you live.

> *"Now then, we are ambassadors for Christ, as though God were pleading through us: we implore you on Christ's behalf, be reconciled to God." (2 Corinthians 5:20 NKJV)*

Beware of False Identities

Christianity is the most prevalent religion in the world. Whether or not every scripture in the Bible represents truth is a debatable topic. However, it does contain undeniable truth as one of the greatest stories ever told about light. (Even if it does include deceptive content inserted unjustly, or if content has been removed.) The greatest story ever told should be the one the Spirit is speaking directly to you. Even the stories we tell ourselves lack spiritual truth, include deceptive content inserted unjustly, or exclude the content of our choosing. Imperfection is the perfect representation of our reality. We can leave perfection to God.

> *"For My thoughts are not your thoughts, nor are your ways My ways, says the Lord. For as the heavens are higher than the earth, so are My ways higher than your ways, And My thoughts than your thoughts."* *(Isaiah 55:8-9 NKJV)*

The corrupt and righteous share the same world. Everything generates a spirit, but not all are godly. **You decide which signs of light are worthy of your attention.** Perhaps the Bible, and everything else, really is exactly as it should be.

> *"Beloved, do not believe every spirit, but test the spirits, whether they are of God; because many false prophets have gone out into the world."* *(1 John 4:1 NKJV)*

KEY POINTS | ASCENSION AS THE HIGHER SELF

- Pursuing a higher level of consciousness to ascend as your higher self requires strengthening your signal connection by continuously seeking the highest power and letting go of any part of life blocking your path toward moving closer.
- A personal connection to—and *your* understanding of—transformational power is key to its effectiveness.
- Your spirit is altered by your interactions with spirits at various levels.
- Interactions will either boost energy or take it away, relevant to the energy levels of the emitter and recipient.
- God is Spirit, love, and the creator of life-giving light energy. Radiating loving light is a godly attribute.
- The consistency of the highest power makes it the primary source to maintain sufficient energy and increase potential.
- You decide which signs are worthy of captivating your attention.

Spiritual Spark Exercise

Think of a trait or circumstance that hinders you from performing as your higher self. Then consider a statement that will increase your strength by moving you closer to spiritual truth. For example, if the opinion of others often sways your decision to act as your authentic self, a counterstatement could be, "I've decided to only focus my attention on information that gives me strength." Make a mental note of your statement and repeat it often with the authority as Director of Energy for your life. **No one else's opinion should have more authority over your life than your own.** Redirecting your energy from negative to positive thought patterns is a form of letting go to allow transformation.

CHAPTER 7

AUTHENTICATING SPIRITUAL IDENTIFICATION

"Then God said, 'Let Us make man in Our image, according to Our likeness ...'" (Genesis 1:26 NKJV)

Ye Are Gods

Are we made in God's image, or have we made God in our image? If we're made in the image of God, we should identify as light gods just as much as human beings. As described in biblical scripture, God is Spirit, love, and light. Hence, God, Spirit, love, and light all denote the same essence. From our father, we inherit these traits. Therefore, it's logical to be considered as light gods and goddesses of the world. **Isn't an heir entitled to the power and identity attributes as stated in the testament?** The Spirit of God is the testator, which Jesus fulfilled the obligation of God's will by sacrificing his life.

> *"The Spirit Himself bears witness with our spirit that we are children of God, and if children, then heirs — heirs of God and joint heirs with Christ, if indeed*

we suffer with Him, that we may also be glorified together." (Romans 8:16-17 NKJV)

The identity traits of the highest power can't be manipulated by man. The authentic traits of your spiritual identity align with this power. Are we gods or merely man? The truth of your existence is gained by a personal experience provided by the Spirit of truth. This can only come from seeking within yourself.

By no means should you blindly accept the concepts that exist in our world without experiencing truth for yourself. Everything outside of you should be looked at with a strong eye of discernment. Deceptive information can be a combination of lies and partial truths, so it appears more acceptable.

"When the Spirit of truth comes, he will guide you into all the truth …" (John 16:13 ESV)

"I have said, Ye are gods; and all of you are children of the most High." (Psalm 82:6 KJV)

"But as many as received Him, to them He gave the right to become children of God, to those who believe in His name: who were born, not of blood, nor of the will of the flesh, nor of the will of man, but of God." (John 1:12-13 NKJV)

"The Jews answered Him, saying, 'For a good work we do not stone You, but for blasphemy, and because You, being a Man, make Yourself God.' Jesus answered them, 'Is it not written in your law, "I said, 'You are gods' '?" (John 10:33-34 NKJV)

"For in Him dwells all the fullness of the Godhead bodily; and you are complete in Him, who is the head of all principality and power." (Colossians 2:9-10 NKJV)

"However, the spiritual is not first, but the natural, and afterward the spiritual. The first man was of the earth, made of dust; the second Man is the Lord from heaven." (1 Corinthians 15:46-47 NKJV)

According to some ancient traditions and Bible scriptures, we are all impressions of God. However, demonstrating the higher qualities of this power is not automatic. According to Christianity, spiritual rebirth is the key to enter the kingdom. You must be aware of the spirit of things and most importantly, the spirit you allow to work through you.

Jesus had to repeatedly defend this ideology. He may be revered now, but he was falsely accused and crucified for who he believed himself to be then. Anyone else that proclaims to do the works of God is also likely to be ridiculed or not taken seriously. **It's difficult to see others beyond how we see ourselves when our comprehension and interpretation of God varies from others.** The people living during the era of Jesus's teachings were just as perplexed when considering man to be God as people are today.

"Jesus answered them, 'I told you, and you do not believe. The works that I do in My Father's name, they bear witness of Me.'" (John 10:25 NKJV)

> *"But although He had done so many signs before them,*
> *they did not believe in Him ..." (John 12:37 NKJV)*

The character of Jesus demonstrated the capabilities of humans with the awareness and level of acceptance to allow the Spirit of God to work through them. Providing us with an example—and the same opportunity—to also be reborn as children of God. **As children of God, we are gods. We wouldn't consider our own children or parents to be something other than what we are.** Seeds bear fruit according to their kind. (Genesis 1:11) The great I Am goes by many names, including ours and the names of everything else in existence. If God is everywhere as everything, what does that make us?

> *"Now when all things are made subject to Him, then*
> *the Son Himself will also be subject to Him who put*
> *all things under Him, that God may be all in all." (1*
> *Corinthians 15:28 NKJV)*

Bodies are still being raised from the dead every day through spiritual rebirth. Jesus was the first, but not the last. His coming was meant to show the way to truth and life by fulfilling God's law and the Prophets. (Matthew 5:17) This means others can follow the same trajectory. The road to spiritual truth and access to abundant power didn't vanish after Jesus. His message is an open invitation to others willing to follow.

Exercising the Power of God

What good is God's power if we can't utilize it? Knowing of a power that doesn't affect your life is useless. **A god is a human attuned to the Spirit of God and consciously using this energy for a divine purpose.** To exercise this power, you must believe it. How else would God be manifested from a formless spirit into physical form if not through its creations? Spirits energize things to react according to the will of the energy source. You are an energized organism. Seeking God's consciousness is a process of liberation from the restrictive bondage that separates you from applying God's power to every aspect of your life.

> "... he who believes in Me, the works I do he will do also; and greater works than these he will do ..." (John 14:12 NKJV)

There isn't a benefit to forfeiting your inherent power from abundant light to primarily focus on your physical aspects. You can think of yourself as a god, or man, or both, or neither, but why not choose the quality of light that provides the perspective of an abundant life? You will face opposition from others no matter what you do or what you believe. Your belief and self-perspective are your own business. There should be mutual respect, allowing others to be without inflicting harm.

"... If they persecuted Me, they will also persecute you ... because they do not know Him who sent Me ... 'They hated me without cause.'" (John 15:20-25 NKJV)

Jesus was the example of the perfect human but was still falsely accused. Everyone is not meant to understand your journey, and most won't. Hate, ignorance, and confusion are to be expected in life. Seeking acceptance from others before making moves can keep you stuck. In this state, the spirit controlling the mind is fear.

"If the world hates you, you know that it hated Me before it hated you. If you were of the world, the world would love its own ..." (John 15:18-19 NKJV)

KEY POINTS | AUTHENTICATING SPIRITUAL IDENTIFICATION

- God, our heavenly father, is the spirit that powers every level of spirits emitted by everything, and God is everything.
- God conceived light that emits life-sustaining energy.
- Your relation to your heavenly father and your biological parents is parent-child. If you are human due to your relation to your biological parents, then you are also a light god due to your relation to God.
- Not claiming your spiritual identity is renouncing a powerful aspect of who you are.

Spiritual Spark Exercise

Take a few minutes to answer the following questions.

1. What does "made in God's image" mean to you? Do you associate the concept with the physical attributes of humans or a formless, invisible force of energy powering man?
2. Do you believe that your DNA has inherited genetic traits from your biological parents and that these traits are within you?
3. Do you believe that your spirit or energy has inherited the light energy traits of God's spirit or God's sun light and that this power is within you?

4. Would you consider your birth parents a different type of being than yourself?

5. As a child of God, do you value your existence as heir of the highest power, or do worldly things determine your view of self-worth?

6. Who are you, and why are you here?

CHAPTER 8

SOLAR-POWERED HYBRID HUMAN

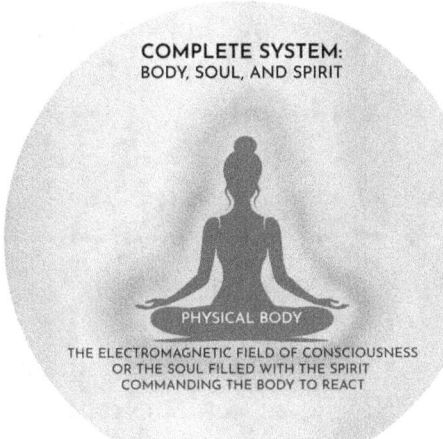

COMPLETE SYSTEM:
BODY, SOUL, AND SPIRIT

PHYSICAL BODY

THE ELECTROMAGNETIC FIELD OF CONSCIOUSNESS
OR THE SOUL FILLED WITH THE SPIRIT
COMMANDING THE BODY TO REACT

**100% DIVINE PERFECTION
MATTER & LIGHT ENERGY**

MADE IN THE IMAGE OF GOD
WITHIN THE SPIRIT OF GOD

SOUL | INDIVIDUAL ENERGY FIELD
EMITS LIGHT ENERGY (RADIATION) AS
INFRARED LIGHT & ENERGY VIBRATIONS

BODY | MATTER + ENERGY
100% MATTER + 100% ENERGY

100% ATOMS, 99.99% ELECTRONS:
• ATOMS FORM THE MOLECULES
NECESSARY TO FUNCTION
• ELECTRONS ABSORB LIGHT ENERGY
FLOWING ELECTRONS ARE ELECTRICITY

CHEMICAL BONDS:
HOLD TOGETHER THE ATOMS THAT MAKE
UP THE MOLECULES FOR THE BODY

THERMAL ENERGY (INFRARED LIGHT) / BODY HEAT:
HEAT GENERATED BY MOVEMENT WITHIN
THE BODY

"You are the light of the world." (Matthew 5:14 NKJV)

The Cause of Light's Effects

Sunlight interacts with everything on Earth. There isn't another light source for our planet that compares to the intensity or range of the sun. Solar power is your primary source of energy. Energy is the ability of an object to move, change, or perform work. Your whole self is a body of matter infused with light (100% matter and 100% energy).

The body, soul, and spirit complete the human electrical system. The soul is the invisible boundary of human consciousness, which unites the mind, body, and spirit to operate cohesively. (While our system may appear as an individual unit, with a godly consciousness, we are all one.). Matter has mass and weight, and our energy component is massless and weightless. The body is the medium that energy employs to do work.

> *"Or do you not know that your body is the temple of the Holy Spirit who is in you, whom you have from God, and you are not your own?" (1 Corinthians 6:19 NKJV)*

Greater clarity of your being can be gained by thinking of existence from an all-inclusive systematic or holistic viewpoint. The family tree of your light system links you to the creator and all things that exists. **Existence is an interdependent system of matter and energy, the seen and unseen.** You can't survive without the elements in your surroundings. Being inseparable makes it a vital part of your system or universal body. The interaction of your electrons with emitted light energy (photons) is your link to all light sources (everything).

> *"For the body is not one member, but many."*
> *(1 Corinthians 12:14 KJV)*

INTERACTION OF ELECTRONS WITH LIGHT

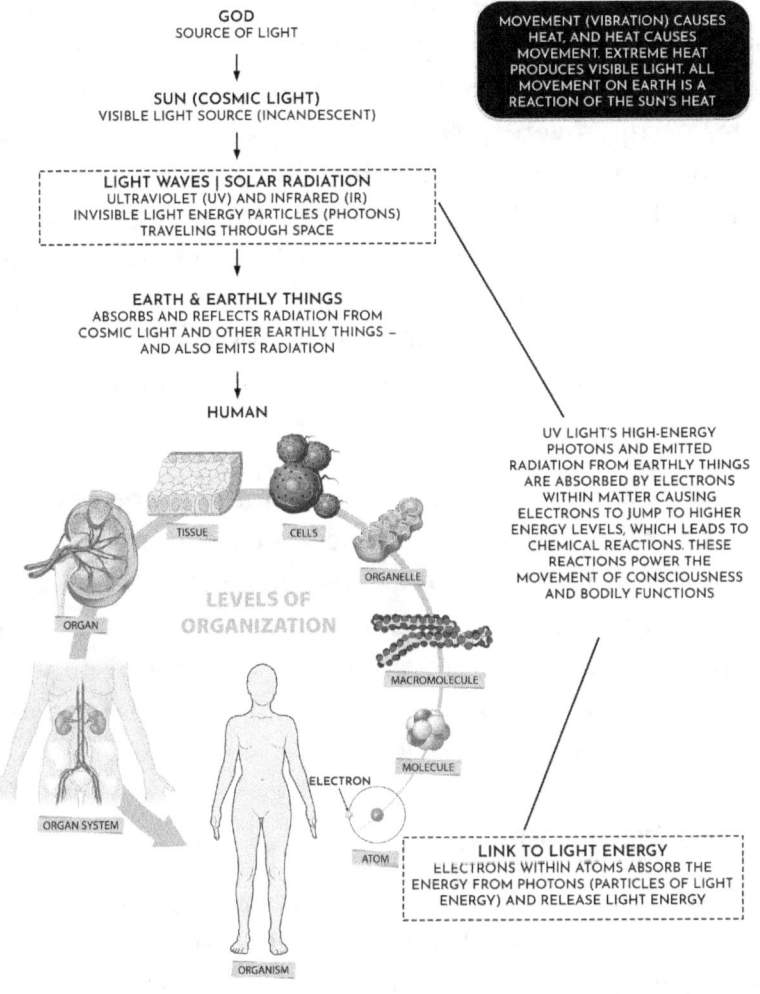

GOD
SOURCE OF LIGHT

MOVEMENT (VIBRATION) CAUSES HEAT, AND HEAT CAUSES MOVEMENT. EXTREME HEAT PRODUCES VISIBLE LIGHT. ALL MOVEMENT ON EARTH IS A REACTION OF THE SUN'S HEAT

SUN (COSMIC LIGHT)
VISIBLE LIGHT SOURCE (INCANDESCENT)

LIGHT WAVES | SOLAR RADIATION
ULTRAVIOLET (UV) AND INFRARED (IR)
INVISIBLE LIGHT ENERGY PARTICLES (PHOTONS)
TRAVELING THROUGH SPACE

EARTH & EARTHLY THINGS
ABSORBS AND REFLECTS RADIATION FROM
COSMIC LIGHT AND OTHER EARTHLY THINGS –
AND ALSO EMITS RADIATION

HUMAN

UV LIGHT'S HIGH-ENERGY PHOTONS AND EMITTED RADIATION FROM EARTHLY THINGS ARE ABSORBED BY ELECTRONS WITHIN MATTER CAUSING ELECTRONS TO JUMP TO HIGHER ENERGY LEVELS, WHICH LEADS TO CHEMICAL REACTIONS. THESE REACTIONS POWER THE MOVEMENT OF CONSCIOUSNESS AND BODILY FUNCTIONS

TISSUE

CELLS

ORGANELLE

LEVELS OF ORGANIZATION

ORGAN

MACROMOLECULE

MOLECULE

ORGAN SYSTEM

ELECTRON

ATOM

LINK TO LIGHT ENERGY
ELECTRONS WITHIN ATOMS ABSORB THE
ENERGY FROM PHOTONS (PARTICLES OF LIGHT
ENERGY) AND RELEASE LIGHT ENERGY

ORGANISM

The smallest particle of matter is an atom, which contains charged particles. Charged particles produce radiation. **Radiation is the light energy we emit, absorb, and reflect.** Nearly 100% of our body is made of atoms. Electrons occupy over 99.9999999% of space within an atom. When light energy is absorbed by the body, electrons within the body absorb the energy, becoming excited to a higher energy level which can trigger various biological processes, such as generating heat, initiating chemical reactions, or in the case of visible light, triggering visual signals in the eye by activating photoreceptor cells in the retina.

You control the inner self but not the internal operations or outer surface layer of your physical body. Automatic bodily functions happen without a conscious thought. However, you *can consciously* redirect your mind to various parts within the body to improve the flow of energy. The inner body may be constantly communicating with you and vice versa, but it has a mind of its own.

The Electrical Current of Life

Radiation, photons, electromagnetic energy, and spirit all relate to light energy. The primary effect of visible light is sight. However, most radiation isn't visible to human eyes.

For example, we don't see heat. Both visible and invisible light energizes the brain by altering the movement of electrons within you. Your entire experience is influenced by the impact.

The spirits emitted by earthly things are like radiation emitted by the sun, but at a lesser intensity. All levels of radiation (spirit) are the same phenomenon with various intensities described in terms of frequency (Hertz), wavelengths (meters), and energy (electron volts). **Spirits are emitted light energy waves that drive the movement of electrons.** The flow of electrons is an electric current. **The state of electrons correlates to life's energy,** like prana (Sanskrit term used in Eastern philosophy) and chi (Chinese medicine term). All electrons in the universe are the same, but the pace of their movement within systems can vary producing different states. Neutral is stable, gaining electrons is beneficial, and losing electrons is harmful.

> *"But Jesus said, 'Somebody touched Me, for I perceived power going out from Me.'" (Luke 8:46 NKJV)*

Charged Particle Imbalance	
Electron Gain (Surplus)	Electron Loss (Deficit)
Negative Charge / Negative Ion	Positive Charge / Positive Ion
Beneficial effects: • reduced pain • better sleep • stress reducer and promotes calmness • regulate chronic illnesses to healthy states • improves blood pressure and flow • speeds healing process • increases energy • relieves muscle tension and headaches	Harmful effects of oxidative stress: • a major contributing factor of cancer production • cellular damage • cardiovascular disease • aging (wrinkles and gray hair) • neurodegenerative disorders • inflammation, the basis for chronic disease • fatigue

Humans primarily lose electrons through the process of oxidative stress. Oxidative stress is internal chaos. It occurs when there is an overproduction of free radicals or a deficiency in antioxidants, leading to an imbalance of electrons in the system. It is caused by the typical stressors, such as toxic environmental factors, lifestyle, poor diet, high levels of stress, medications, and chemical reactions within the body. Neglecting to restore your energy is also a factor.

A loss of electrons can lead to cell and tissue damage contributing to aging and disease development. Losing electrons is losing vital energy. **Electrons are the fundamental particles sustaining life at the cellular level**.

Balancing the Body

The interaction of sunlight is the primary cause of free electrons on Earth's surface. Grounding or earthing may stabilize your electrical system by absorbing these free electrons. Sunning also has many benefits as the regulator for many bodily functions. The free flow of energy when exposed to sunlight, Earth's surface, large bodies of water, fresh air, and space can instantaneously soothe your senses, calming your mind and body. (Conversely, walls and ceilings are energy barriers in all aspects of life.) The five elements of nature (fire, earth, water, air, and ether or space) are all natural healers under certain conditions.

Our modern lifestyles have almost eliminated replenishment by nature from our daily routine. Your primary source of electrons is food (chemical energy). Oxygen allows the flow of those electrons to generate energy within your body from the food you eat.

Sunlight powers the water cycle. The interaction of water molecules with electrons inside the body is crucial for many biological processes. The human body is composed of 50-75% water. Drinking pure water itself does not readily provide electrons because it is neutral in that state. Water intake from our food sources participates in chemical reactions that involve the transfer of electrons. Water could also be enhanced to provide electrons by adding a small amount of sodium (but too much sodium could cause health issues) or other electrolytes.

KEY POINTS | SOLAR-POWERED HYBRID HUMANS

- Your experience is based on the light energy you emit, absorb, and reflect.
- The interaction of particles of light energy (photons) and electrons within you is your link to everything in the universe.
- The primary source of radiation on Earth is from the sun.
- Absorbed and emitted light energy is the spirit of things.
- Light energy is a result of moving electrons within the atoms of an object, which has a reactive effect that triggers the movement of electrons within other objects.
- Absorbed light energy is transferred to the atoms within your body, causing movement.
- The movement of electrons within your body is your electrical current.
- Electrons are the fundamental particles sustaining life at the cellular level.
- The state of your electrons affects your emitted spirit and health.
- Positive ions (a loss of electrons) are at the root of most health issues.

Spiritual Spark Exercise

Although we don't generate our own energy like the sun, each of us operate like mini solar systems on Earth's surface. You exist in a field of countless stars. You're the star in the center of your world. Your experiences, circumstances, values, personality traits, physical attributes, and possessions are the orbiting objects. The light you radiate into the world, is influenced by, and has attracted the conditions involving the people, places, and things of your experience.

The light sources you give your attention are drawn closer to you. The sun is the most powerful light, but the maximum benefit of any source can only be gained by understanding its power and fully exposing yourself through a direct connection. The spirits of the things closest to you have the highest impact on your life regardless of their energy level, but your energy level at the time of interacting is also a factor.

Take a moment to reflect on the solar system created by your gravitational pull. Do you recognize the type of spirits you want to emit reflected off the objects orbiting around you? Acknowledge your role in attracting the surrounding circumstances. This exercise is not to find fault or take pride, but rather recognize the powerful effect of your energy. Are there areas of life that the gravitational pull of others is causing you to follow their system versus your own?

PART II

ENERGY IS INFORMATION

CHAPTER 9

HARNESSING YOUR LIGHT

Tuning into Transformational Light

Spiritual and physical signals are received and transmitted through the same field. There is no separation but rather invisible light energy pervading the entire universe and working through things that are detectable by your physical sense receptors.

The retinas of your eyes can't reflect things that aren't within your field of view. The same concept applies to your other sense receptors. You understand that when a person, place, or thing is no longer within range to be detected by your physical sense receptors, the subject still exists. However, the connection to continue perceiving a sign of the subject is lost. The same goes for your spirit or mood.

If something isn't accessible by your current frame of mind, it's as if it doesn't exist. For example, if the light of transformational power isn't your current focal point or stored within your mind, you won't see signs of yourself transforming. The absorbed energy from your experiences makes impressions that are stored away until a set of conditions are met causing them to resurface. Like stored funds in a bank account. You can only take out what you've put in. When a transaction linking to the account is made, the remaining balance is altered. If you deposit transformational power, you'll be able to use it towards transforming.

There are a ton of spirits all around you. A wide range of scenarios are always occurring around the globe with the corresponding energy being absorbed by the people involved which causes them to react. The events receiving your attention are the ones that will affect you. To embody the required energy traits for the life you want to live, you must tune your attention to the things with qualified spirits to power your will with the desires, intentions, thoughts, emotions, and behavioral reactions related to your desired experiences. By doing so, this energy is absorbed and deposited into your spiritual account then exchanged for the fulfillment of your desire.

Everything has an energy level, whether it appears lively or not. Your consciousness can elevate and expand into heaven, while the body has limitations. Physical death or a near-death experience is not a requirement to experience heaven or activate levels of consciousness that reveal spiritual truth. Heaven is an energetic state of consciousness accessed by directing your attention to the highest power. Your mind can travel to the Big Bang and back to Earth transformed by the brightest light if you allow it to go there.

Energy is a vital component of life regardless of your level of awareness. With awareness, you can redirect your energy to better serve your intention. **We are all tuned into different sources of information with experiences corresponding to that level of energy.** Each person will view the same scene from a different physical and mental perspective.

The information you take notice of is demonstrated through your behavior and lifestyle. Internal stimuli are from substances within the body or mind. This could be thoughts, emotions, or chemical reactions within the body. External physical stimuli are sensed as smell, taste, touch, sight, or sound. Your perspective or state of being when processing a stimulus will determine its effect on your energy level. Your world is shaped by your unique perception of it.

Creating Heaven on Earth

Heaven isn't easily accessed from a physical standpoint, but you can always look up to see the field of heavenly light. You can experience the presence of God and heaven on Earth by paying attention to the signs of heavenly things. **Considering heaven as a faraway destination without means of transportation to get there, other than dying, will not draw it any closer to you in this lifetime.** The only thing standing in your way of being empowered by a limitless force is your lack of understanding of who you are, how you function, and your true relation to the source. Your mind will expand as far as your limitations permit. Access to heaven is within you.

Upon entering this world, you become identified as the physical body. It remains the primary basis of your identity until spiritual truth is ignited. You can become attached to your external status, but status will change. You may be labeled as a certain type of person based on the attributes of your mood or emotions, but they are only phases. Your mood and status represent temporary states of being.

Who you are shouldn't be confused with status, moods, or your physical possessions. Who you are stems from your divine nature as Director of Conscious Energy for the organism you're assigned. The spirit you radiate is based on the information you direct your mind to. A director's role can be challenging—especially when you aren't aware of your position.

Unhealthy reactions, including thoughts, could indicate that you are temporarily veering away from your true potential and spiritual truth. The illusory separation between yourself and heaven will begin to dissipate as you move closer to the light. Trying to master or change something or someone other than yourself before having a basic understanding of who you are and how you function demonstrates your level of ignorance.

Imitators of Light

Once you understand the basics of your system, you start to recognize the similarities in all existing systems. Your creative works mirror the fundamental designs of nature. The functionalities of digital information apps are somewhat replicas of the human mind, and wireless communication devices emit light energy (radiofrequency radiation). Online searches are another example. Once you input information to search, the feed of results and suggested content will continue to automatically populate according to the keywords of your search and your response to the results.

The same concept applies to the mind. You are constantly inputting information and responding. You remain clueless about the things that don't receive your attention. Your next move will relate to the conditions you created by your previous moves.

When you are focused on a particular target, everything else happening around you is temporarily withdrawn from your conscious mind. You will start to reflect the qualities of the higher self when the information you focus on reflects these qualities. You will start to reflect the qualities of a healthier person when the information you focus on reflects these qualities. You will start to reflect the qualities of a wealthier person when the information you focus on reflects these qualities. You will start to appear as a suitable candidate when the information you focus on and present to others reflects these qualities.

To change your mental energy, **you must imitate the spirit you want to reflect by directing your attention towards**

qualified energy sources capable of providing what you need in return. If you continue following the auto-suggested cues from the environment, a drastic change may never occur. A conscious redirect with a specific target is a tactic for harnessing the light to produce the results of a desired experience.

> *"Therefore be imitators of God as dear children. And walk in love, as Christ also has loved us and given Himself for us ..." (Ephesians 5:1-2 NKJV)*

KEYNOTES | HARNESSING YOUR LIGHT

As the director of your conscious energy, you have the power to redirect your focus to things that relate to the energetic state you desire. Continuously uplifting your spirit trains the mind to pay attention to signs associated with similar experiences.

Spiritual Spark Exercise

View your search or watch history feeds for social media, internet, and entertainment applications. Does the information relate to elevating mental energy or improving your physical status, or is it general information unrelated to your life's intentions? Also consider how your routine activities improve your quality of life.

CHAPTER 10

SIGNS OF LIGHT

"And there shall be signs in the sun, and in the moon, and in the stars ..." (Luke 21:25)

All Sensations Are Signals

Despite the estimated 200 billion-trillion stars, outer space appears dark. Although light energy is weightless, massless, and invisible, it travels through space as a signal carrying information that reflect the quality of the emitting source. All signals convey messages.

A photon is the smallest particle of light. Light travels as electromagnetic waves that vibrate. Vibrations are signs of light energy. We detect physical and energy signals by our physical sense receptors or as chemical stimuli. Spirits are stimuli providing the energy for chemical reactions. Light energy waves supply the necessary information for a particular purpose. Each spirit gives the command for corresponding reactions. And all your sensations are signs of light communicating messages converted to a scene allowing you to see, taste, touch, smell, hear, think, and comprehend. **Your willpower, desires, intentions, thoughts, emotions, and behavioral reactions are shifted by the quality of absorbed spirits.**

Incoming and outgoing light energy travels through space as electromagnetic waves. The light energy absorbed by your body is converted to an electrical signal. Electrical signals are processed in the nervous system as the root of all physical and mental activity carrying the commands for your system to function.

Electromagnetic waves travel at the speed of light through empty space for an infinite distance until absorbed by something. Astronomers observe and collect data from light energy waves emitted by celestial objects. Everything speaks the universal language of vibration.

The unique sign of light that you emit into the world is called your electromagnetic signature or spectral signature. This signature is like a spiritual fingerprint. **The most fundamental message of any sign is the existence of the thing communicating the sign.** You are a sign of existence amongst many other messages that you convey. You are a source, emitter, and receiver of light energy or spiritual signals.

INCOMING ENERGY
ALL SIGNALS FROM THE ENVIRONMENT
& INTERNAL CHEMICAL STIMULI ARE ENERGY
SIGNALS CONVERTED TO SENSATIONS TO PERCEIVE REALITY

ALL EXPERIENCES ALTER YOUR ENERGY FLOW

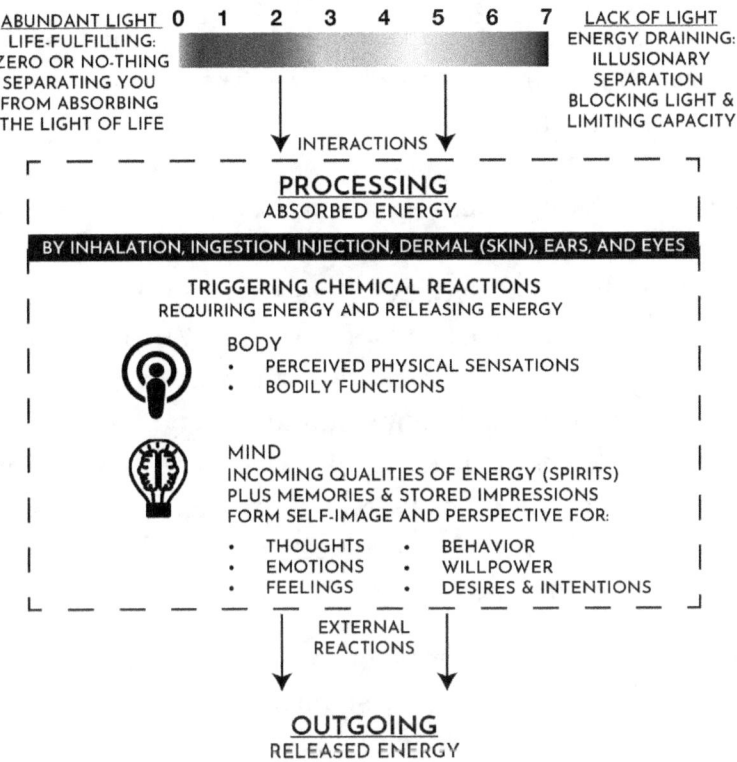

| ABUNDANT LIGHT | 0 | 1 | 2 | 3 | 4 | 5 | 6 | 7 | LACK OF LIGHT |

ABUNDANT LIGHT
LIFE-FULFILLING:
ZERO OR NO-THING
SEPARATING YOU
FROM ABSORBING
THE LIGHT OF LIFE

LACK OF LIGHT
ENERGY DRAINING:
ILLUSIONARY
SEPARATION
BLOCKING LIGHT &
LIMITING CAPACITY

▼ INTERACTIONS ▼

PROCESSING
ABSORBED ENERGY

BY INHALATION, INGESTION, INJECTION, DERMAL (SKIN), EARS, AND EYES

TRIGGERING CHEMICAL REACTIONS
REQUIRING ENERGY AND RELEASING ENERGY

BODY
- PERCEIVED PHYSICAL SENSATIONS
- BODILY FUNCTIONS

MIND
INCOMING QUALITIES OF ENERGY (SPIRITS)
PLUS MEMORIES & STORED IMPRESSIONS
FORM SELF-IMAGE AND PERSPECTIVE FOR:

- THOUGHTS
- EMOTIONS
- FEELINGS
- BEHAVIOR
- WILLPOWER
- DESIRES & INTENTIONS

EXTERNAL
REACTIONS

OUTGOING
RELEASED ENERGY

PHYSICAL EXPRESSIONS:
BEHAVIORAL ACTIONS
VITAL SIGNS

BYPRODUCTS:
WASTE/ TOXINS, CARBON DIOXIDE,
DEAD SKIN CELLS, BLOOD, SWEAT AND TEARS

RADIATION:
HEAT (THERMAL ENERGY OR INFRARED LIGHT)
SPIRIT "VIBE" VIBRATIONAL FREQUENCY OF LIGHT ENERGY WAVE

Seeking Sends a Signal

Seeking is a signal to God, and your transformation is evidence of God's response.

> *"But you shall receive power when the Holy Spirit has come upon you; and you shall be witnesses to Me ..."* *(Acts 1:8 NKJV)*

When you seek something it sends an energy signal as a request for information about the subject you're seeking. Your energy signal is your emitted spirit. Spirits command a response from the receiver of the signal. When you direct your energy towards something a response is guaranteed. For instance, directing your mind to a friend will produce thought patterns related to that friend. A unique vibrational pattern will be converted to physical sensations or thoughts about the related subject. This is why memories can trigger emotions.

The vibrational frequency of your spirit and the vitals of your body are authentic signals of your physical and energy states. (Which is why a lie detector test is used in addition to verbal testimony in some cases.) The energy of your system is attuned to the spirits you pay attention to in each moment. It's not that you are exhibiting the behavior of the spirits you're observing, but your energy is temporarily captivated and altered by whatever you choose to notice.

"My sheep hear My voice, and I know them, and they follow Me." (John 10:27 NKJV)

There is always an inner voice commanding a reaction, but it isn't always from the highest level of spiritual power. The voice is usually your own under the influence of the absorbed spirits. All levels of the spirit can convey commands through the vibrations of energy signals that trigger reactions. The source of a spirit can be identified by its energy attributes. God's voice may be the vibration of all light energy as the spirit of everything, but godly attributes reflect the highest light.

Only the highest level of positive energy can strengthen your willpower to function at maximum potential, ensuring optimal health for a life of abundance, as intended. A godly spirit produces vibrations forming mental impressions that command radiating life-giving light.

Information gained by spiritual truth is beyond the limitations of your individual consciousness and external experiences. Your connection to the field of collective consciousness is an inheritance from light. The messages from any level of spirit will continue to flow if you remain an open channel to receive the signals.

"But we have this treasure in earthen vessels, that the excellency of the power may be of God, and not of us." (2 Corinthians 4:7)

Answering the Call

Seeking sends a signal, and answering the call is following the commands of the sought spirit's response. Increasing your energy capacity makes you a suitable candidate for a higher calling. The call is simply the implanted ideas by the spirits interacting with your energy field (soul). You're always receiving and transmitting calls. A self-imposed question is, 'Who are the subjects on the other end of the line?'

Exposing the mind to things that elevate your awareness, in turn, aligns you with circumstances requiring the application of your expanded knowledge. You pay attention to subjects related to your interest. This is the basis of frequency tuning.

The signal you cast by seeking calls everything which orbits around the light of your life. To attract new things, redirect your vibrational signal by paying attention to things that will move you and your energy attributes closer to acquiring what you want.

A qualified spirit precedes the things you desire because it provides your ability to change things. As you pay attention to the things you want and what's required to get them, you are also absorbing the energy aspects. Once adequate attention is paid, you are the new owner of the sought after energy traits.

If you're having trouble fulfilling a desire, your spirit might be unintentionally calling unqualified recipients that are unable to produce what you are hoping for in return. Create an intention to redirect your calls. You receive the conditions that relate to your spiritual callings.

KEYNOTES | SIGNS OF LIGHT

Being aware that everything is a sign of light that can alter your electrical current, gives you the power to redirect the energy of your life toward the energetic states you desire to experience. You can move through life more mindful of internal and external stimuli while minimizing or maximizing their effects on your energy levels.

Spiritual Spark Exercise

Everything is a sign. Some events demand our attention, but there are many things that we willingly direct our attention to. Even the seemingly insignificant signs that trigger reactions are either steps toward your life's intentions or distractions. Standing still is a slow motion descension unless you are elevating consciousness while seeking clarity for the next move. The accumulated steps of past experiences led to this moment.

Note something that you did in the past twenty-four hours to elevate any aspect of your life. Make sure it's not something that maintains current conditions. Then, note one thing within the same timeframe that could be viewed as a distraction or sign of procrastination.

CHAPTER 11

QUALITIES OF LIGHT

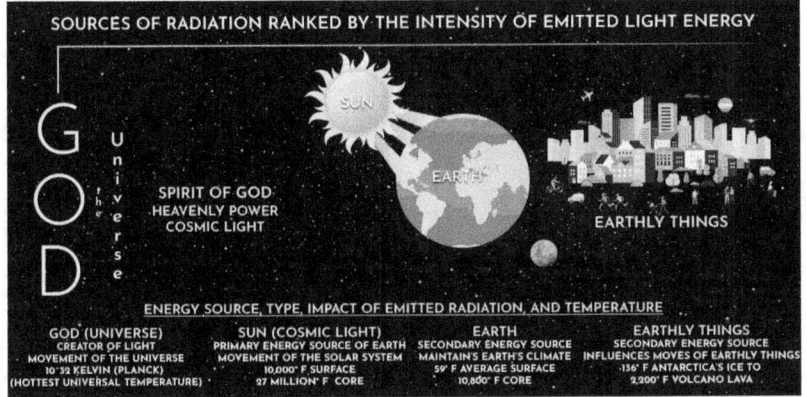

SOURCES OF RADIATION RANKED BY THE INTENSITY OF EMITTED LIGHT ENERGY

GOD
Universe

SPIRIT OF GOD
HEAVENLY POWER
COSMIC LIGHT

SUN

EARTH

EARTHLY THINGS

ENERGY SOURCE, TYPE, IMPACT OF EMITTED RADIATION, AND TEMPERATURE

GOD (UNIVERSE)	SUN (COSMIC LIGHT)	EARTH	EARTHLY THINGS
CREATOR OF LIGHT	PRIMARY ENERGY SOURCE OF EARTH	SECONDARY ENERGY SOURCE	SECONDARY ENERGY SOURCE
MOVEMENT OF THE UNIVERSE	MOVEMENT OF THE SOLAR SYSTEM	MAINTAIN'S EARTH'S CLIMATE	INFLUENCES MOVES OF EARTHLY THINGS
10^32 KELVIN (PLANCK)	10,000° F SURFACE	59° F AVERAGE SURFACE	-136° F ANTARCTICA'S ICE TO
(HOTTEST UNIVERSAL TEMPERATURE)	27 MILLION° F CORE	10,800° F CORE	2,200° F VOLCANO LAVA

From Lack to Light

"And He is before all things, and in Him all things consist." (Colossians 1:17 NKJV)

The energy of God's Spirit, cosmic light, your light, and everything else in the world are one and the same *but a different quality*. Light and darkness are opposite levels of the same force. There is energy and a lack of energy, or strength and weakness, and ultimately life and death. Every aspect of existence is within this range.

"There is one body, and one Spirit, even as ye are called in one hope of your calling;" (Ephesians 4:4)

God is a man-made term used to reference the creator of light. The reactions caused by the interactions of light energy and matter created the universe. Regardless of how energy is used, it's still God's light. On the other hand, godly acts represent the quality of life-giving light.

ENERGY CHARACTERISTICS BASED ON THE QUALITY OF ABSORBED LIGHT

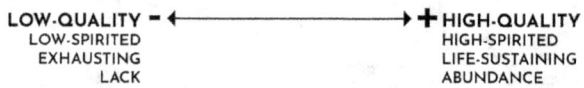

LOW-QUALITY	HIGH-QUALITY
LOW-SPIRITED	HIGH-SPIRITED
EXHAUSTING	LIFE-SUSTAINING
LACK	ABUNDANCE

GENERAL ENERGY ATTRIBUTES

DEFICIENT	SUFFICIENT
RESTRICTING	FREE-FLOWING
DANGEROUS	SAFE
DEPLETING	RESTORING
UNPRODUCTIVE (POTENTIAL)	PRODUCTIVE (KINETIC)

BELIEFS, MORALS AND VALUES

ADOPTED PERSPECTIVES	SEEKER OF HIGHER POWER
EXTERNAL POWER SOURCES	INHERENT INNER TRUTH
LIMITED IMAGINATION	LIMITLESS IMAGINATION

IDENTITY

IDENTITY CRISIS	SELF-REALIZATION
IMITATOR OF WORLDLY IDOLS	AUTHENTIC (HIGHER) SELF
CARNALLY MINDED	SPIRITUALLY MINDED

PHYSICAL HEALTH

DISEASE	OPTIMAL PERFORMANCE
INTERNAL CHAOS	INTERNAL STABILITY
TIRED	ENERGETIC

HABIT PATTERNS

REMAIN A CONSTANT	PROGRESSIVE GROWTH
SELF-DESTRUCTING	SELF-HEALING
WEAK-WILLED	STRONG-WILLED

DECISIONS

CONFINING & CONSTRICTIVE	LIBERATING & EXPANSIVE
UNINFORMED OR IGNORANT	INFORMED OR WISE

While your body is progressing towards expiration, your spirit can be renewed to become more alive with the quality of godly light. **The spirit of your perspective will either position you closer to self-realization or further away towards an identity crisis.**

Electromagnetic Spectrum of Radiation (Light)

As "the light of the world," the fundamental information of the full light spectrum is useful. The full electromagnetic spectrum of radiation has seven types of light, but you can only see one. Therefore, there are tons of invisible energy waves all around you being emitted by everything. The collective spirit fills the universe.

Since light energy waves are invisible, they are commonly referenced as spirits. Although we cannot see this energy, it may cause a reaction if there's an interaction. Our eyes are attuned to see primary light sources that produce their own light, such as the sun and stars, and the light reflected off objects that don't produce their own visible light. We also observe light energy in motion as it works through us and the objects within our environment, which the ability to move, change, or transform is inherited by absorbing light energy.

ELECTROMAGNETIC SPECTRUM OF LIGHT ENERGY (RADIATION)

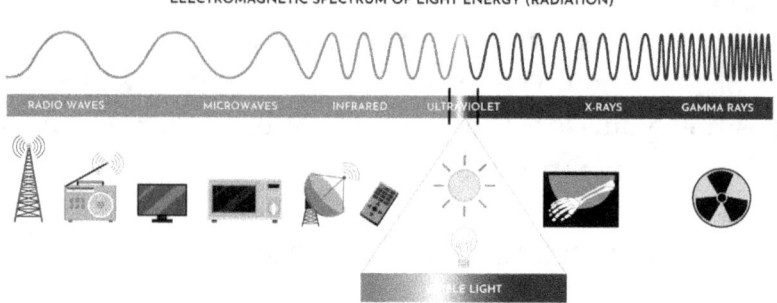

VISIBLE LIGHT (ENERGY) SPECTRUM
RANGE DETECTABLE BY THE HUMAN EYE

LONG WAVELENGTH/
WEAK SIGNAL

SHORT WAVELENGTH/
STRONG SIGNAL

WAVELENGTH

625-750 nm	590-625 nm	565-590 nm	500-565 nm	485-500 nm	450-485 nm	380-450 nm
RED	ORANGE		GREEN	BLUE	INDIGO	VILOLET
400-480 THz	480-510 THz	510-530 THz	530-600 THz	600-620 THz	620-670 THz	670-790 THz

FREQUENCY

LOW FREQUENCY/
LESS ENERGY

HIGH FREQUENCY/
MORE ENERGY

According to the US Department of Energy, the entire rainbow of light observable to the human eye only makes up a tiny portion of the electromagnetic spectrum of about 0.0035 percent. In addition, the portion of the universe that we can directly observe accounts for less than 5%. The remaining 95% is referenced as dark matter and dark energy.

The electromagnetic field (EMF) is the space throughout the universe in which light travels. The individual field surrounding each object and the emitted light energy collectively creates the universal field, and it's generated by the electric current of matter. You can't see the EMF (also known as a biological field) that surrounds and permeates your physical body.

The EMF is a defense mechanism acting as an invisible shield of protection, like the EMF of Earth, the geomagnetic field, and the magnetosphere. The strength of your shield is determined by the quality of your consciousness. The power to make decisions that improve your life is strengthened as you increase your energy potential.

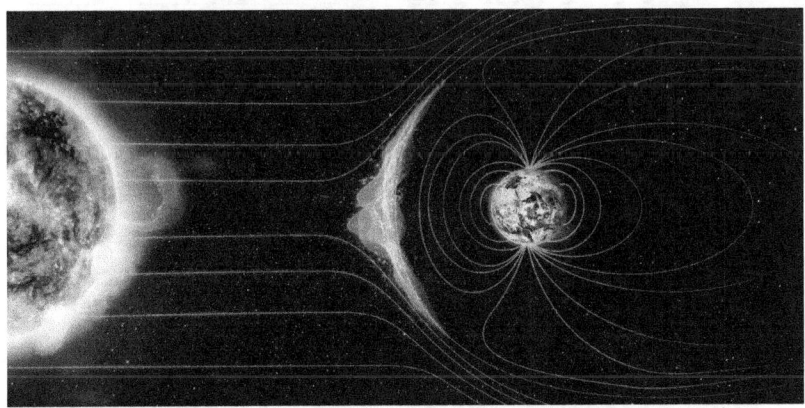

Aura Layers and Aspects of Consciousness

The aura is the energy field surrounding your physical body, also referring to the EMF or energy field of the soul. There are ancient traditions that believe the human aura consists of seven layers. Each layer of the aura correlates to a chakra. Energy from your environment interferes with your aura. Chakras are the energy vortexes that move energy through your body. Meridians are the electrical wiring and network. What's more, the chakras and auras pertain to various levels of consciousness. As we move up the ladder of consciousness, we dissolve the barriers that block the energy flow necessary for enlightenment.

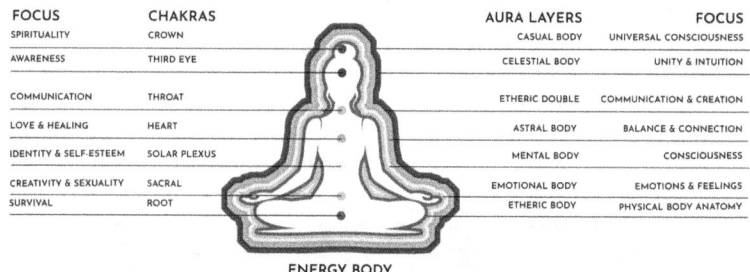

FOCUS	CHAKRAS		AURA LAYERS	FOCUS
SPIRITUALITY	CROWN		CASUAL BODY	UNIVERSAL CONSCIOUSNESS
AWARENESS	THIRD EYE		CELESTIAL BODY	UNITY & INTUITION
COMMUNICATION	THROAT		ETHERIC DOUBLE	COMMUNICATION & CREATION
LOVE & HEALING	HEART		ASTRAL BODY	BALANCE & CONNECTION
IDENTITY & SELF-ESTEEM	SOLAR PLEXUS		MENTAL BODY	CONSCIOUSNESS
CREATIVITY & SEXUALITY	SACRAL		EMOTIONAL BODY	EMOTIONS & FEELINGS
SURVIVAL	ROOT		ETHERIC BODY	PHYSICAL BODY ANATOMY

ENERGY BODY

Godly and Worldly Spiritual Light

In biblical text, godly spirits are fruits of the spirit, and worldly spirits are acts of the flesh. Fruits of the Spirit are yielded by performing godly acts of radiating positive light, and the acts of worldly spirits are self-serving and lack light.

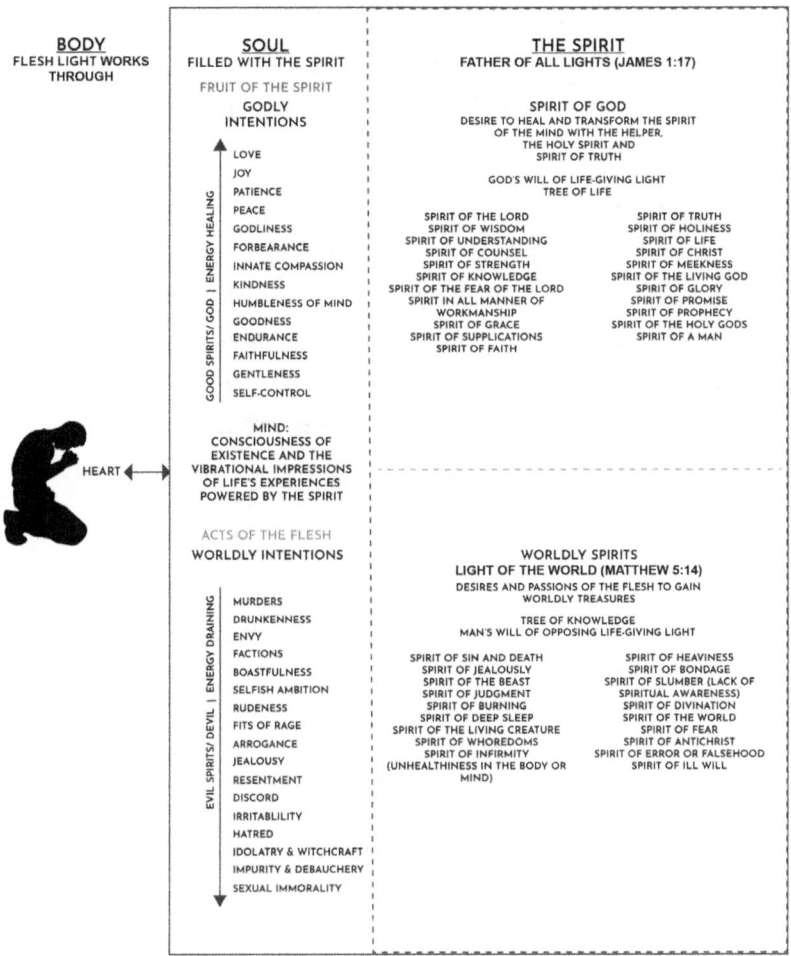

BODY	SOUL	THE SPIRIT
FLESH LIGHT WORKS THROUGH	FILLED WITH THE SPIRIT	FATHER OF ALL LIGHTS (JAMES 1:17)

FRUIT OF THE SPIRIT

GODLY INTENTIONS

GOOD SPIRITS/ GOD | ENERGY HEALING

- LOVE
- JOY
- PATIENCE
- PEACE
- GODLINESS
- FORBEARANCE
- INNATE COMPASSION
- KINDNESS
- HUMBLENESS OF MIND
- GOODNESS
- ENDURANCE
- FAITHFULNESS
- GENTLENESS
- SELF-CONTROL

SPIRIT OF GOD
DESIRE TO HEAL AND TRANSFORM THE SPIRIT OF THE MIND WITH THE HELPER.
THE HOLY SPIRIT AND SPIRIT OF TRUTH

GOD'S WILL OF LIFE-GIVING LIGHT
TREE OF LIFE

SPIRIT OF THE LORD	SPIRIT OF TRUTH
SPIRIT OF WISDOM	SPIRIT OF HOLINESS
SPIRIT OF UNDERSTANDING	SPIRIT OF LIFE
SPIRIT OF COUNSEL	SPIRIT OF CHRIST
SPIRIT OF STRENGTH	SPIRIT OF MEEKNESS
SPIRIT OF KNOWLEDGE	SPIRIT OF THE LIVING GOD
SPIRIT OF THE FEAR OF THE LORD	SPIRIT OF GLORY
SPIRIT IN ALL MANNER OF WORKMANSHIP	SPIRIT OF PROMISE
SPIRIT OF GRACE	SPIRIT OF PROPHECY
SPIRIT OF SUPPLICATIONS	SPIRIT OF THE HOLY GODS
SPIRIT OF FAITH	SPIRIT OF A MAN

MIND:
CONSCIOUSNESS OF EXISTENCE AND THE VIBRATIONAL IMPRESSIONS OF LIFE'S EXPERIENCES POWERED BY THE SPIRIT

HEART ←→

ACTS OF THE FLESH

WORLDLY INTENTIONS

EVIL SPIRITS/ DEVIL | ENERGY DRAINING

- MURDERS
- DRUNKENNESS
- ENVY
- FACTIONS
- BOASTFULNESS
- SELFISH AMBITION
- RUDENESS
- FITS OF RAGE
- ARROGANCE
- JEALOUSY
- RESENTMENT
- DISCORD
- IRRITABLILITY
- HATRED
- IDOLATRY & WITCHCRAFT
- IMPURITY & DEBAUCHERY
- SEXUAL IMMORALITY

WORLDLY SPIRITS
LIGHT OF THE WORLD (MATTHEW 5:14)
DESIRES AND PASSIONS OF THE FLESH TO GAIN WORLDLY TREASURES

TREE OF KNOWLEDGE
MAN'S WILL OF OPPOSING LIFE-GIVING LIGHT

SPIRIT OF SIN AND DEATH	SPIRIT OF HEAVINESS
SPIRIT OF JEALOUSLY	SPIRIT OF BONDAGE
SPIRIT OF THE BEAST	SPIRIT OF SLUMBER (LACK OF
SPIRIT OF JUDGMENT	SPIRITUAL AWARENESS)
SPIRIT OF BURNING	SPIRIT OF DIVINATION
SPIRIT OF DEEP SLEEP	SPIRIT OF THE WORLD
SPIRIT OF THE LIVING CREATURE	SPIRIT OF FEAR
SPIRIT OF WHOREDOMS	SPIRIT OF ANTICHRIST
SPIRIT OF INFIRMITY (UNHEALTHINESS IN THE BODY OR MIND)	SPIRIT OF ERROR OR FALSEHOOD
	SPIRIT OF ILL WILL

"Now the works of the flesh are evident, which are: adultery, fornication, uncleanness, lewdness, idolatry, sorcery, hatred, contentions, jealousies, outbursts of wrath, selfish ambitions, dissensions, heresies, envy,

murders, drunkenness, revelries, and the like; of which I tell you beforehand, just as I also told you in time past, that those who practice such things will not inherit the kingdom of God.

But the fruit of the Spirit is love, joy, peace, longsuffering, kindness, goodness, faithfulness, gentleness, self-control. Against such there is no law. And those who are Christ's have crucified the flesh with its passions and desires. If we live in the Spirit, let us also walk in the Spirit. Let us not become conceited, provoking one another, envying one another." (Galatians 5:19-26 NKJV)

KEY POINTS | QUALITIES OF LIGHT

- Your quality of life and well-being are primarily dependent on the awareness of your energy aspect.
- The qualities of the information from everything you process forms your perspective.
- The qualities of incoming energy signals and your current energy levels determine the qualities of your impressions to perceive, understand, and participate.

Spiritual Spark Exercise

Spiritual (energy waves) and physical signals trigger electrical impulses that are processed as information relayed to the brain to perceive and understand existence. Not only do you exchange energy with other people and things, but there is also an energy exchange with each experience. For example, the qualities of your spirits are infused into your work. Your attitude, skills, perspective, creativity, thoughts, work ethic, emotions, and self-worth are a few energy attributes that could become apparent qualities of your projects. You are also stimulated by your work, which is essentially self-talk.

Reading this book is an experience with an energy exchange. Why did you decide to read this book? Recall the signals that attracted your spirit to the spirit of this book. Has your interpretation of light energy shifted?

CHAPTER 12

INTERPRETING LIGHT

"For the kingdom of God is not in word, but in power."
(1 Corinthians 4:20)

The term used to reference the force that created the power permeating all things is irrelevant. You can use the word that resonates as the most powerful to you. The name could be expressed verbally or non-verbally. God is Spirit, not human. **The universal language of God speaks to and through all things as vibrations.** Vibration is the inherent language of light. The word of God is power from God, providing the ability to move, create, and be all things that are possible.

Everything in the universe is always moving or vibrating because all things are a mass of atoms that are constantly in motion. As humans, our feelings emit a distinct vibration when we focus our attention on God or a higher power. Your vibration is also what others sense from you, regardless of your actions or the words flowing from your mouth.

Interpreting the concept of the highest power for yourself is the most important decision you make in your lifetime. Yet so many people adopt the beliefs of the most influential people around them without question, without seeking within themselves at any point, or without further exploration of alternative concepts. Most don't even study the adopted beliefs for themselves. They simply take the words of others for a limited, blind-faith approach.

It would be wise to carefully select the governing rules and standards that you are allowing to dictate your entire life. The ideas that you accept associated with God and your personal interpretation of this information influence your acceptance of others and your response to the world. To gain clarity, you should research the origin, history, and intention of any doctrine for yourself. The best option would be to seek within first. Your inner self has direct access to truth and wisdom.

"These things indeed have an appearance of wisdom in self-imposed religion, false humility, and neglect of the body, but are of no value against the indulgence of the flesh." (Colossians 2:23 NKJV)

If your belief isn't powerful enough to move you toward a healthier lifestyle, then it's permitting you to perform unhealthy acts. It's not that the power of God is insufficient to transform you; rather, you have inserted so many layers between you and God. To remove the layers that distance you, you must understand what you have subscribed to, along with an everlasting will and love to prioritize practices that cultivate this ideology.

You can't expect an unplugged appliance to work just because electricity dwells within the infrastructure of your home. Simply knowing of and having access to this power doesn't mean you are or will be charged by it. Likewise, a membership with a group of religious people doesn't grant automatic faith and an instant attainment of a god-like consciousness. Recharging requires a direct connection to the power source. Reprogramming yourself to a new set of beliefs takes patience. This is not a part-time or short-term practice. However, you are fully in charge of your way of pursuance. Your commitment level is directly related to the output.

If your spirit is in a weakened state of hopelessness and you are unable to establish a personal connection with God for yourself, it's alright to start with a system of beliefs by accepting a recommendation from someone you trust. They could also be welcomed to pray on your behalf. Immediately after gaining enough strength, you should seek answers from your intuition. It's also alright to change your mind about what you believe. As you grow, your perspective could change.

An interpretation of truth should not be forced upon others but simply shared to shed light with those that express an interest. The notion of seeking within would cease to exist if you were meant to be a follower of someone else's way.

> *"God is my strength and power: and he maketh my way perfect" (2 Samuel 22:33 KJV)*

KEYNOTES | INTERPRETING LIGHT

Interpreting the force that created light is a solo experience of going within yourself to directly connect with the light particles within you. Just like your DNA, there is embedded information that travels with light. Divine power provides a perfect understanding crafted for each one of us, relevant to our level of consciousness. Your understanding continues to grow as you continue to seek the truth of existence. There are many powerful stories from others, but none will compare to your own experience.

Spiritual Spark Exercise

The silent vibrations of your impulses are heard throughout the field of light. God's word is power. Power is your energy, and your energy is radiated as a signal conveying information. If you are seeking a truth message and have not been able to hear the response, speak with your infused emotions and listen to your energy shifts. Take note of changes in thought patterns and your mood. Communicating with God is an exchange of energy that your brain will interpret into information that you understand. The energy to feel uplifted or make a positive change is a response.

CHAPTER 13

YOUR WAY IS THE WAY

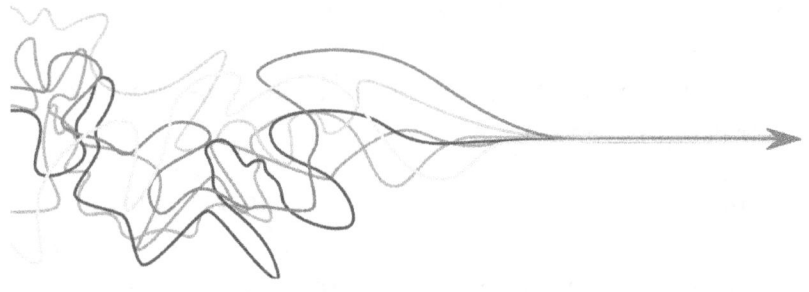

"But seek first the kingdom of God and His righteousness, and all these things shall be added to you." (Matthew 6:33 NKJV).

"... behold, the kingdom of God is within you." (Luke 17:21 KJV)

"Ask, and it shall be given you; seek, and ye shall find; knock, and it shall be opened unto you: for everyone that asketh receiveth; and he that seeketh findeth; and to him that knocketh it shall be opened." (Matthew 7:7-8 KJV)

There are many helpful techniques and practices geared towards becoming an enlightened or righteous person. The truth is, neither of these methods are the way, but rather a way. There is no right or wrong way to self-realization. Looking outside of yourself may cause confusion. **Every path of seeking within yourself leads to one and the same truth.** There is only one origin of creation. Whichever path you decide to take, it is surely the one necessary for your growth. Your way will unfold one moment at a time as you navigate through all the lessons required for your progression.

There will be a degree of variance even if two or more people are following the same belief system. You can mix and match practices as you see fit for you. Each soul is allowed to find liberation without the judgment and scrutiny of others. This freedom comes from giving yourself permission to live life according to your authentic desires.

Nothing outside of you has the power to liberate your mind. Authenticity is derived from the creator. There is a bigger picture at play that no one can perceive for another—no matter how righteous one may be. We can barely find our way through life. We were not appointed as authority figures of other souls.

There are spiritual bonds connecting you to specific roles that align with your innate gifts. Your assignments in life are based on your unique experience. Divine links cannot be broken. If you have the will, there is a way. You can choose whichever path is more effective at elevating your consciousness toward your higher self.

You can accept or reject any information based on what feels right for you —no matter who or what organization is providing the content. There is a ton of misleading information about anything and everything. As you continuously make a personal connection, you will be guided along the pathway that is mapped out just for you. Eventually, you will be able to transcend well beyond the comfort zone of your present characteristics. This is when you fully begin to comprehend the Bible scripture, "you must be born again" (John 3:1-21) because you experience the scripture for yourself as you become more spiritually attuned.

"Enter by the narrow gate; for wide is the gate and broad is the way that leads to destruction, and there are many who go in by it. Because narrow is the gate and difficult is the way which leads to life, and there are few who find it." (Matthew 7:13-14)

KEYNOTES | YOUR WAY IS THE WAY

There are many resources to help you along the journey of self-improvement. At a certain level, the training wheels must come off and you walk the path that is lit for you. You have an internal guide.

Spiritual Spark Exercise

Sitting quietly, take three deep breaths as you acknowledge your internal guide and the power that flows through your being.

PART III

THE COST OF PAYING ATTENTION

CHAPTER 14

SPIRITUAL CURRENCY

Life Is the Sum Total of Paid Attention

Time is a variable outside of your control. You can't manage time itself. Time will pass regardless of what you do or don't do and will continue to do so long after you're gone. Time measures moments of existence in relation to one another. Each moment is filled with actions, change, or movement. It's not a matter of time, but rather the events of each moment that will move you in a particular direction.

Strong willpower comes at the cost of your attention. Your attention is an asset you must carefully manage. Life is pricey, and you pay for everything with your attention. It is required to participate in life. The currency exchanged in any event is energy. Life is the currency we all have, regardless of what's in the bank. **Paying attention is spending your life one moment at a time.** Paying attention is a spiritual exchange. How you use your energy will determine the course of your life.

You're directing mental energy to information processed as electrical impulses.

Paying attention is taking notice of any signal that creates an observable sensation. Every sign conveys information. If the information you pay attention to isn't in alignment with your intentions, you may be using your most valuable asset on something that isn't worth the price. The deposits, withdrawals, and balance of life's energy are shown by your state of being and how you conduct yourself in this world. You can't make a direct deposit for more moments to extend life, but you can do things to sustain a healthy life filled with intentional moments.

Your values should align with your intentions. Values can help you determine which events are worthy investments of your attention. You wouldn't haphazardly spend money on things you don't consider to be a worthy exchange. Anything you willingly pay attention to should be worthy of your energy.

Your focus should involve how to effectively use and replenish your energy. There is no line of credit. You can't borrow someone else's lifeline. The implications of your interactions with spirits are relevant to your energy balance. Therefore, the events of the world will affect each person differently. You either have sufficient energy to handle the situations that arise, or you don't. Bankruptcy of vital life force is death.

Awareness Is Power, Money Is a Resource

Authentic power is the invisible force that moves all things. Your power isn't dependent on money —although an uplifted spirit can be inspired to make an unlimited amount of money. Your relation to the source of authentic power determines your ability to accumulate and use the resources available to you. Material possessions and money may be the ultimate power gauge for many, but neither will elevate consciousness or provide nutrients. However, they can be useful resources to obtain these things. **The circulation of worldly currency sustains a healthy economy, but the electrical current of your being sustains life.**

> *"And you shall remember the Lord your God, for it is He who gives you power to get wealth ..." (Deuteronomy 8:18 NKJV)*

A desire to overpower or control others is an indication of a belief that it is necessary to disempower others to gain power, much like the idea that someone must lose for you to win, not realizing that the ultimate power is within each of us. If your primary source of power is obtained by resources such as money, assets, or through controlling other people, you will feel powerless when you lack any of these. There is nothing wrong with accumulating material possessions or acquiring assets, but they are not the basis of your authentic power or your identity.

> *"For those who live according to the flesh set their minds on the things of the flesh, but those who live*

according to the Spirit, the things of the Spirit. For to be carnally minded is death, but to be spiritually minded is life and peace." (Romans 8:5-6 NKJV)

Money is man-made. The power of consciousness is spiritual currency from the creator. Wealth in this spiritual account creates habits leading to optimal health, peace, a mindset of abundance, authentic love, joy, excitement, and enlightenment. A sound mind is priceless. Priceless is more valuable than any amount of money.

The most valuable treasure isn't accumulated through the physical experience. It's the associated spiritual reaction. It's revealing the inherited qualities of consciousness and maximizing the potential to apply the power. Spiritual gifts can't be bought with worldly currency. And they can only be realized with awareness and multiplied by strength. Therefore, awareness of your power is the ultimate currency.

"'Whoever drinks of this water will thirst again, but whoever drinks of the water that I shall give him will never thirst. But the water that I shall give him will become in him a fountain of water springing up into everlasting life.'" (John 4:13-14 NKJV)

KEYNOTES | SPIRITUAL CURRENCY

You pay for everything with an asset more valuable than any amount of money. Your attention is paid for every experience. Your attention is moments of your life directed towards a particular subject. Moments of life are made possible with energy. Paying attention to anything is an energy exchange with the subject of your attention. In other words, exchanging parts of your life to receive the energy emitted from the subject of your attention. Like exchanging parts of your life to earn income. We often ask the question, "How much will something cost?" A question to consider going forward is, "Will this experience be worth a part of my life?"

Spiritual Spark Exercise

- Make a list of the things you may be holding onto that aren't a worthy exchange of your life's energy.
- At the end of the list, write the following statement: "The things I have listed are no longer worthy of my mental or physical energy. This sheet of paper is where I leave them. I now set myself free as they are no longer worthy of my concern."
- Safely burn the paper over a sink, in a cooking pan, or another fire-resistant area.
- Take a moment to honor your inner strength as the gatekeeper of your life's energy.

CHAPTER 15

THE WILL OF POWER

The Garden of Eden Is Your Mind

The Garden of Eden is your mind. Physical and spiritual signals are the two methods to obtain information. Both forms of information are essential parts of life. Information from the Spirit of God is represented by the Tree of Life. The Tree of Knowledge of Good and Evil is information associated with the spirits of worldly things, which aren't all bad.

The Tree of Life is spiritual truth about existence gained by a direct connection to the highest power. It's the silent vibrational messages of life-giving light energy. The fruit from this tree draws us closer to God's will and our innate characteristics. This fruit provides healthy positive energy and seemingly supernatural powers. It's the source that helps you achieve the highest levels of awareness.

The Tree of Knowledge of Good and Evil is a combination of opinions, lies, misinformation, and interpretation of truth from worldly spirits and the associated physical experiences. Evil relates to mental and physical actions in the opposite direction of reflecting positive life-sustaining light. It's a combination of God's will and free will at varying proportions. The fruit from this tree provides a range of energy. Low-level fruit causes self-destruction over time. To save yourself from this trajectory, you must eat more from the Tree of Life.

The strength of your will to be, do, have, and feel is determined by the will you accept and apply. The will is your energy. The qualities of your energy derive from the powering source. Willpower stimulates electrical impulses or internal signals that drive decisions.

Every possibility is made possible by the same light. All wills derive from the same origin. All external information is a secondary resource related to God's will for your life. Information from external sources can be beneficial, but interpretations of information from others are crafted from and for *their* understanding. Shared experiences can spark thoughts that lead you towards your own understanding.

High-quality Light Is Life

> *"All things were made through Him, and without Him nothing was made that was made." (John 1:3 NKJV)*

God's laws, the laws of nature, and universal truth pertain to energy. The principles of energy don't apply to a particular era, person, place, or thing. It is pertinent to the collective body, hence, applicable to everything (light sources).

There is a purpose for your portion of the light. Each part of the whole is essential for completion. We all fall somewhere within the gray. No matter where you land, you're still light. Even if the level of light is closer to darkness.

Opposing God's will has consequences. Sometimes, we subject ourselves to these situations—even when warning signs are heeded. The force of nature may allow the event to happen, but you are responsible for the predicament. Lessons don't always have to be learned the hard way. However, each experience provides an opportunity to go through the emotions and grow through the lesson which, in hindsight, will reveal itself as a blessing.

> *"Let every soul be subject unto the higher powers. For there is no power but of God: the powers that be are ordained of God. Whosoever therefore resisteth the power, resisteth the ordinance of God: and they that resist shall receive to themselves damnation."* *(Romans 13:1-2)*

Pain and suffering subside the closer you are to the light. The light is God's will. This light illuminates options you can't see in the dark and provides a glimpse of heaven on Earth with a sense of liberation or elevation. A life in alignment with the highest power produces a different perspective. It's not that unpleasant things will no longer happen, but rather, your shield of protection can withstand an attack. Your internal world can remain intact even when the material world is at war.

Life and every other state of being are temporary. By acknowledging this fact, you can accept and allow things to pass through and out of your system without an intense attachment to them. Burdens come from the weight of worldly things. Light energy is massless and weight-less. **Each new breath allows the opportunity to expand, release, and remember that everything that happens is within the field of God's light.**

> *"Take my yoke upon you, and learn of me; for I am meek and lowly in heart: and ye shall find rest unto your souls. For my yoke is easy, and my burden is light." (Matthew 11:29-30)*

KEYNOTES | THE WILL OF POWER

Your will is your energy, and power is associated with the sources of your energy. Your willpower reflects the energy qualities of the sources you have accepted to power your being. To be, do, have, and feel what you desire requires the corresponding energy levels to achieve it.

Spiritual Spark Exercise

Visualize waking up tomorrow with all the qualities of your highest self and living your ideal life. Imagine all aspects of this life in detail. Then, write the vision of your full day in a schedule format or summary to include the following:

- the time you wake up
- your morning routine
- what you eat throughout the day
- who you are spending time with
- what you are wearing (clothes, jewelry, fragrance, etc.)
- where you are going
- how you earn income
- how much you earn
- where you live
- what your rituals are to strengthen the mind and body
- what time you go to bed

What do you feel when you imagine your life this way? Does your current schedule reflect dedication to embody the energy qualities of the highest power or more of the same energy to attract the same conditions currently surrounding you?

CHAPTER 16

BYPRODUCT OF PAID ATTENTION

"As obedient children, do not conform to the evil desires you had when you lived in ignorance. But just as he who called you is holy, so be holy in all you do ..." (1 Peter 1:14-15 NIV)

Spirits are sensational forces that spark emotions, producing pleasant and unpleasant feelings. Nothing gets paid more attention than our desires to do, be, have, or feel something. You don't desire experiences that have never crossed your mind. Desires are crafted by the things you have paid attention to and then identified as something you'd like to experience. They can compel you to redirect your energy flow toward the desired reality. **Desires are internal signals linked to your spirit's will to be, do, have, and feel.** Therefore, your desires are influenced by the characteristics of stored impressions from your experiences and the incoming spirits you absorb and process as part of yourself.

The attributes of your power sources determine the intensity of your willpower. A weak will is associated with a weak connection to high-spirited things that can shift your energy towards intentional living. For example, if most of your attention is placed on the Spirit of God, the will of God powers your will. In this case, the impulses of your desires are associated with fulfilling experiences related to God's will. God being the most intense power source means the willpower is also strong. Then your energy is directed towards the intention of doing God's will.

Our intentions pave the way to fulfill desires. Desires along with willpower stimulate continuous movement towards your intended path. Willpower is strengthened by focusing on the things that support the desired experience. Desiring an experience but focusing on conflicting messages weakens willpower. For example, wanting to eat healthier, but giving your attention to advertisements and recipes of unhealthy foods will produce cravings for the unhealthy food. The strength of your willpower is the strength of your magnetic power to attract what you desire.

Desires should support wellness. There are depictions of unhealthy habits portrayed as normal. Many indulge in them without realizing the consequences until there are signs of an issue. **As you ascend, what is considered normal for others may no longer be acceptable for you.** Your higher self makes decisions in alignment with optimal health. The energy you consume and emit should shift from satisfying temporary physical sensations to events that deposit life-sustaining energy.

The desire to transcend current conditions with more money, loving relationships, or possessions is natural. A desire isn't necessarily about the people, places, or things that are involved. Nor is it about being, doing, or having something you want, but more so, how these things can make you feel.

Emotions are internal motions signaling change from one state of being to another based on events as they are happening. Feelings are emotions processed from your perspective in which you can recall the feeling with thoughts at any time without the actual event recurring. You crave the sensation you think you'll get from attaining what you desire. You ultimately want to experience the chemical reaction that produces an elevated state of being that changes the perspective of your physical conditions, status, and identity characteristics.

You are connected to infinite power. You sense your ability to expand beyond your physical conditions and mental limitations. This feeling will never be fully satisfied by things that are limited and temporary. You will always want more because a part of your being is limitless. Reuniting with the Spirit of God fills you with the energy necessary to fulfill your healthy desires and disregard others.

Desires are a necessary motivating force to act. However, you can learn to become content whether a particular condition is met or not. When you don't have, or can't get, what you strongly crave, you can become mentally unstable.

Every moment has an ending. All sensations will come and go. Every sensation you experience transpires within you as a chemical reaction. You can decide whether to express gratitude for all you have or disappointment for the few things you don't have. Accessing internal power reveals that the most valuable things in life are inherently yours.

> *"Delight yourself in the LORD, and he will give you the desires of your heart." (Psalms 37:4 ESV)*

KEYNOTES | BYPRODUCT OF PAID ATTENTION

Your desires derive from your willpower, and your will is powered by the things you pay attention to and accept as desirable experiences to obtain a particular sensation. You are attracted to the spirit of things. Physical and spiritual signals cause chemical reactions that are accompanied by a feeling. Fulfilling your desires is achieved by continuously redirecting your energy to the activities that strengthen your spirit to progressively move forward.

Spiritual Spark Exercise

All desires require a change to occur before they become a reality. Otherwise, they would already be fulfilled. This involves shifting your physical and mental energy towards the things you desire. By doing so, you absorb the necessary energy traits that will cause you to react in favor of manifesting the desire. Essentially, strengthening your willpower. Even if it's simply walking to the fridge to get the food you crave. That action requires the same steps as fulfilling any other desire.

Five Steps of Crafting and Fulfilling Desires

1. **Pay attention** to life and decide what you want based on the limitless possibilities.
2. **Identify a desired experience.**
3. **Create the intention** to achieve the experience.

4. **Strengthen willpower** by directing energy towards, or paying attention to, things that ignite an impulse in support of fulfilling the desired experience.

5. **Fulfill the desire** by having the experience.

What is your greatest desire? Are you focused on things with spirits that support this desire? Reference the steps above to fulfill any desire.

PART IV

OVERCOMING THE PROGRAMMING TRAP

CHAPTER 17

SETTING THE INTENTION TO RISE

Setting an intention for living gives rise to purpose and purpose to rise above any situation or the opinion of others. **Intentions point to the path of least distractions to guide your attention towards the target.** A compelling intention serves as the harmonizer of your existence. It's a way to fulfill your desires and inspirations.

> *"The heart of man plans his way, but the LORD establishes his steps." (Proverbs 16:9 ESV)*

Your vision should be so enormous that transformational energy from the highest power is required. It is the pathway to embodying your higher self. It shouldn't be influenced by external conditions. The closer you align yourself with God, the feeling of trying to control everything or allowing yourself to be controlled by others will dissipate. You can focus on your part and allow others to work on theirs. Whatever happens is one of many possibilities.

"And we know that all things work together for good to those who love God, to those who are the called according to His purpose. For whom He foreknew, He also predestined to be conformed to the image of His Son, that He might be the firstborn among many brethren." (Romans 8:28-29 NKJV)

Authentic Is Perfect

At the beginning stages of life into early adulthood, most of us are heavily influenced by our environment. As we journey through our own understanding of existence, we begin to make a shift according to the standards of who we are versus who we thought we had to be to fit into society. We shift from the mindset of the masses to the master of our mind while disregarding social norms. We can gradually detach ourselves from the life we created under the pretense of a false identity. How we gauge our progress in life is now based on the intentions we've set.

If you are following the standards of anyone other than yourself, you may appear to be above average on one scale but at the lower end on another. As the standards change, you are subject to try and keep up with the trends. There is no one to compare yourself with and nothing or no one to follow when the target is your authentic self—not even the internal component we call the perfectionist. Rather than the idea of *becoming something*, you can be your authentic self while continuing to uplift your spirit and infuse the qualities into your projects.

Perfection is divine nature, not human nature. This concept could relieve the pressure of attempting to do what naturally occurs by God's design. Rather than perfection, you can focus on continuous improvement in all areas. Accepting who you are and shining your unique light is a decision. If you are perfect by nature's design, being authentic is the perfect expression of your inner self.

Anything required for your divine assignment is gifted through your growth. The best time to start something is whenever you decide to start. You can start with the will to fulfill your assignments to the best of your ability. If being yourself is the ultimate target, all you need to do is let go of the false identity traits that block access to your inherited power.

We're all in the process of starting something to fulfill a desire—whether it is starting something new, starting over, renewing, being reborn, resetting, repurposing, or reinventing a part of life. You already are and have what it takes to be and do all that you desire. That's why you have the vision. To minimize mistakes along the way, you can be prepared for your assignment. You're empowered by the spirit of your choosing to be who you are in each moment. The assignment and how it's done comes with the appointing spirit.

Lifelines Not Deadlines

Intentions don't have milestones with deadlines. It's different from a goal or result. An intention serves as a compass indicating a direction you have chosen for your life. It's your lifeline to overcome obstacles. It's not about making it to a destination at a particular time. It's about creating a life filled with moments that are in alignment with the intention. Every moment of your life is a small fragment of an accomplishment. Each day is as worthy of your gratitude and celebration as any other.

The key component of an intention is identifying the destination and heading in that direction. Distance, timing, or reaching the destination isn't fully in your control. **If God is truly behind the wheel of your will, you don't really know the distance or timing, and the destination could be a much better place.** The spirit prepares you for the assignment, you don't always get an itinerary prior to starting.

You don't know if your remaining time on Earth will allow you to go the full distance to reach the destination. However, every moment provides an opportunity for you to head in that direction. Where you leave off, someone else could be assigned to continue. Your body is temporary, but the spirit working through you isn't. Your journey is about continuous progression along the path God has set before you.

"A man's steps are of the Lord; How then can a man understand his own way?" (Proverbs 20:24 NKJV)

An accumulation of moments with actions supporting your intention will inevitably lead to where you are meant to be. You are subject to the laws of nature as a part of a massive system. When a particular set of conditions are met, what happens is beyond your control. You can work with the outcome by accepting it and moving along. You don't need to focus your attention on when events will occur. If you are doing all you can, that is all you can do.

Intentions last a lifetime and can be adjusted along the way. Deadlines are helpful for certain projects, but setting strict deadlines for divine assignments can interfere with God's plan. There is nothing wrong with creating plans or setting deadlines, but if they aren't completed by the anticipated time, you shouldn't falter. Unforeseen factors of co-existence are bound to occur. We are only co-creators. We don't rule the world. In every equation, you play a small but significant part.

"Do you not believe that I am in the Father, and the Father in Me? The words that I speak to you I do not speak on My own authority; but the Father who dwells in Me does the works." (John 14:10 NKJV)

Results are not due to setting deadlines or goals. Invisible forces go before you to lay the foundation. We are oblivious to the interconnected workings of any event, yet we play a role in someone else's vision, as others do in ours. The magnitude of your impact reaches people you may never know or meet. Setting a target date doesn't guarantee fruition. In other words, things will happen according to nature's way and timing, regardless of your plans.

You can practice trusting the process. The traditional way of planning by a clock and calendar is combined with aligning yourself to inspirational energy. The details of the next step will be revealed as the present step comes to completion. Energy naturally flows. You don't have to worry about tomorrow when you know the force behind each moment. Intentional living and divine timing become your lifeline.

> *"For grace you have been saved through faith. And this is not your own doing; it is the gift of God, not a result of works; so that no one may boast. For we are his workmanship, created in Christ Jesus for good works, which God prepared beforehand, that we should walk in them."(Ephesians 2:8-10 ESV)*

KEYNOTES | SETTING THE INTENTION TO RISE

An intention acts as a powerful guide that points you in the direction of materialized imaginations. It serves as an invitation to welcome Wisdom and Truth to meet you where you are and lead you where you're meant to be under the influence of a higher power. Your unique path unfolds one step at a time, and it can never be retraced.

Setting deadlines is a great tactic for certain projects. However, divine assignments don't usually come with deadlines because the people who are appointed by God humbly devote their remaining life to the work. The spirit does the work through you by assigning roles according to your commitment. What you see in divine imagination is specifically designed for you with all your circumstances considered. At the right time, in the right way, the assignment will be completed.

Spiritual Spark Exercise

Review your existing life's intention or create a new one based on your current level of consciousness. You can revise it at any time. Below are questions that can assist with developing a powerful intention:

a. What is the ultimate feeling that I desire to achieve, and why is this so significant?

b. What do I want from this life and why?

   c. What do I want to contribute to this life?

   d. What impression of light am I meant to express?

   e. Which topics energize my mind, body, and spirit the most when spoken, heard, read, or visualized?

CHAPTER 18

REWRITING THE CONSTITUTION OF A PROGRAMMED MIND

"The light of the body is the eye: if therefore thine eye be single, thy whole body shall be full of light. But if thine eye be evil, thy whole body shall be full of darkness. If therefore the light that is in thee be darkness, how great is that darkness!" (Matthew 6:22-23 KJV)

The Foundation

Your perspective controls your experience. Initial perspectives are usually derived from external experiences with a lack of spiritual awareness. In this case, the world forms your ideas of self-image and a worldly viewpoint. Although this perspective may serve you well for the beginning stages of your life, over time, this can become a distorted view. Once a certain level of maturity and your basic needs are met, self-development can initiate the inward journey toward self-realization.

You've chosen your standpoint to view the world based on the information you've gathered, accepted, and identified as applicable to your experience. You can't underestimate the psychological impact of historical events, government authority, religion, personal experience, your upbringing, and family traditions. These factors constitute the programming of your mind. They also play a major role in the current conditions around the globe.

Most of the information that went into your programming may have been gained without harmful intentions; however, there is also misinformation meant to manipulate you. Your experience can plant seeds in your subconscious mind that you don't even realize are there. As you align with spiritual truth, some of your deeply rooted ideas may start to conflict with your emerging identity.

The personality traits created by your environment serves a significant purpose. Some aspects of your personality were created as basic survival characteristics or defense mechanisms to avoid being hurt mentally, emotionally, or physically. **Some traits have now become the obstacles preventing you from letting go of adverse thoughts to accept new favorable possibilities.** You can observe your interactions to determine where a transformation may be warranted.

The impressions made in the mind of a child can have a lifelong impact. The experiences from childhood have shaped who you are today. At some point, it would be worthwhile to revisit your inner child with the strength of your adult perspective to offer any necessary self-healing or seek guided therapy.

Your inner child needs to know she or he is now safe, protected, loved, and valued. This can be a liberating step if it hasn't already been taken. Having a direct link to a higher power and self-care practices that strengthen your mind allow you to not only reclaim your genuine identity but to be more empowered in all that you are and do.

The Power of Systems

An authentic form of higher power is not to control you but to liberate and keep the unity of the Spirit in the bond of peace. (Ephesians 4:3) Many people have suffered and are suffering from planted seeds of oppression based on physical conditions outside of their control. You have a certain degree of free will. You decide what is meaningful and valuable to you based on personal preference. Your preferences shouldn't be applied to other people or their possessions.

The current power dynamics of this world were shaped by greed for power and wealth. The government was not created to serve and protect us, but rather to control, conform, and prohibit the people from rising to retaliate. War or division due to differences is not the will of God working through man. The French Wars of Religion lasted thirty-six years. War is man's will. The scheme of war is never freedom or peace.

The governing systems and leadership around the globe were created in the aftermath of numerous wars. The winners made the rules in favor of their protection with the dynamics to override the laws and enforce them on the masses. The deceitful people working as religious leaders and governing authorities are responsible for many corrupt systems in existence today. There may be good people in many of these positions, but some of these organizations were founded by (and still include) biased individuals with ill intentions.

> *"Put on the whole armour of God, that ye may be able to stand against the wiles of the devil.*
>
> *For we wrestle not against flesh and blood, but against principalities, against powers, against the rulers of the darkness of this world, against spiritual wickedness in high places." (Ephesians 6:11-12)*

We are all uniquely different. **All standards, suggestions, and recommendations should only be used as a reference directed by your internal guide.** Systems can be helpful, but systems that cause chaos or division can do more harm than good for the collective whole. Trying to reform a system that wasn't formed by us may not be the best use of your energy.

All man-made systems or institutions are someone's business. Most are created for financial gain. Large systems created for the masses will benefit some while serving as a hindrance to others. If the terms of an existing system don't suit your needs, there are usually other options to consider. You can educate yourself on the existing systems to maximize their benefits or create your own system.

Reclaiming Your Power

To rewrite the fundamental principles of your programming, you must take full accountability and responsibility for your current position. You made the decision to download all the information stored in your mind. Then, it was processed to build the life you have. That same information from your life is also uploaded to the same collective pool of identity characteristics and lifestyles available for anyone to download and install.

Deceitful leaders and other misinformed people are not to blame for your circumstances. By understanding their role, you can find strength in your inner power to overcome the restraints. Instead of resentment, you can have compassion for the ignorant acts of others. **Being humble involves acknowledging that we all operate from a certain level of ignorance due to a lack of wisdom.**

Free spirits seek the guidance of inner truth. Manipulated minds will easily follow the way of other people or the established systems. Sometimes without any questions. A person strongly influenced by external power will continue to blame external factors as the source of all their circumstances, causing them to remain powerless in their affairs and dependent on the systems they despise. **If we're still blaming others for our current circumstances, at what point do we take responsibility for our present to shape our future?**

Your Past No Longer Exists

Your past no longer exists. However, it does influence the present, but history is not repeating itself. History is recorded, replayed, and then projected by your mind into the present. You use valuable energy from the present moment to ponder on a phantom event. You could objectively view the past to move forward with a clean slate instead of rehashing unfavorable conditions.

Moments come and go like your next breath. **Thoughts of the past or future should be used to inspire you, not drain you.** Despite all that has happened in your past, you are still here. Regardless of what will be, you can make it through. The worst-case scenario is death, which is an inevitable part of living. If the past is keeping you stuck, perhaps you should leave it where it is and move on. Likewise, if thoughts of the future are causing anxiety, you should stay in the present moment. Easier said than done, but why use your mind to torment yourself?

"That which has been is what will be, That which is done is what will be done, And there is nothing new under the sun." (Ecclesiastes 1:9 NKJV)

There is truly a reason for everything. All that has happened has been allowed because it's a possibility of existence. It was within the laws of nature and bound to occur with a particular set of events. Whether consciously or unconsciously aware, every experience is interconnected, dating back to the beginning of time.

God made the first move, and the universe has been reacting ever since. Our response becomes the cause for another person's reaction with a never-ending wave cycle. This is the nature of energy transferring from one form to another. You can learn to let go and receive renewed energy.

"'All things are lawful,' but not all things are helpful. 'All things are lawful,' but not all things build up. Let no one seek his own good, but the good of his neighbor." (1 Corinthians 10:23-24 ESV)

KEYNOTES | REWRITING THE CONSTITUTION OF A PROGRAMMED MIND

Your observations of how other people behave in various settings caused you to adopt similar traits, form habits, and identify as members of the various groups you've participated in. Some of your traits were developed as a coping mechanism. As you experience truth for yourself, new traits and habits emerge, and some of the existing ones no longer apply. Embracing your authentic identity allows you to gradually regain control over certain aspects of your life. The mind is liberated to form ideas in favor of the life you want to create for yourself once you start deleting obsolete programming input by others.

Spiritual Spark Exercise

In the exercise at the end of "The Will of Power" chapter, you imagined the qualities of your higher self and your ideal life. What are the conflicting beliefs or ideas about yourself or others that separate you from living that life now? Note ways to bridge the gap by applying your intention.

CHAPTER 19

ENERGY HEALING

"... the god of this world has blinded the minds of the unbelievers, to keep them from seeing the light ..."
(2 Corinthians 4:4 ESV)

Healing Is Energy Restoration

The soul is the temple, dwelling place, or container of our mind and body which is pervaded by the energy attributes of the powering spirit. The most effective treatment for restoration is filling the soul with the highest spirit. Every function of the body is dependent on the quality of your energy levels. Sunlight is still free. There isn't a power source on Earth more intense than sunlight. The sun's energy is the primary and natural regulator of the human body.

Homeostasis is the state of balance among all the body systems needed for the body to survive and function correctly. In homeostasis, the body's levels of acid, blood pressure, blood sugar, electrolytes, energy, hormones, oxygen, proteins, and temperature are constantly adjusted to respond to changes inside and outside the body to keep them at a normal level. **Light energy drives the master clock within the hypothalamus, which is the main regulator of homeostasis in the body.** The quality of chemical energy from food is the other major factor of homeostasis. As hybrids, we must have the proper measure of energy and supporting conditions for the spirit and body.

Self-healing Is the Opposite of Self-destructing

You have the power to heal or harm yourself with the energy you decide to absorb. People have more belief in their ability to self-destruct than self-heal. If you can do one, you can do the other. **Self-healing is sustaining energy, and self-destructing is depleting it.**

The belief of our capabilities is inherited from the spirits of our power sources. We must believe we're healers to embody the characteristics to make healthier decisions. If we don't believe that changing our habits will make a difference, we won't be motivated to change. Self-healing is a conscious act to raise our energy towards healthier levels.

Some people aren't aware that the body generates electricity, so energy healing is often regarded as an alternative treatment when an energy imbalance is often the root cause (unless it's a physical wound). The body heals itself, but its ability to do so is subject to the conditions you provide. Therefore, your role is to provide the best quality energy and conditions for healing. Doctors don't heal people. They perform procedures and prescribe medications, which could also be viewed as a measure of providing the best conditions for the body to restore itself.

High-quality food, supplements, and prescriptions are beneficial healing aids to address part of your energy imbalance, but those options target the physical body and trigger chemical reactions that may not have a long-term effect if they don't eliminate the root cause. Your energy needs recharging like your electrical devices. You need to rest and plug into a higher power until you are recharged. Then repeat often. Sleep isn't enough, and the quality isn't always restful.

Radiant Spirits Restore Light

An energy healer is someone or something that transfers positive energy from one source to another to restore balance. Like an energy transfusion serving the same purpose as a blood transfusion, but for energy replenishment. This could be done by any method of harnessing the light of positive spirits. The person in need of healing may not be in a mind-frame to accept the situation with positive thinking. The high-spirited presence of a healer might uplift, encourage, and console the person being treated. Most of us have noticed an energy boost from the interaction of a high-spirited person, whether in person, over the phone, or by thought.

We have been programmed to believe more in the power of man-made healthcare systems, including pharmaceuticals, than natural elements. A lack of faith was the reason Jesus gave when his disciples asked why they couldn't cast out a demon. **By God's design, we each have spiritual gifts. By man's systems, we have been dulled by a lack of faith.** You can't radiate power that you don't believe you have.

> *"Then the disciples came to Jesus privately and said, 'Why could we not cast it out?'"*
>
> *So Jesus said to them, 'Because of your unbelief; for assuredly, I say to you, if you have faith as a mustard seed, you will say to this mountain, "Move from here to there," and it will move; and nothing will be impossible for you.'" (Matthew 17:19-20 NKJV)*

As part of human nature, even the most attuned person is subject to needing someone else to assist with their healing process. No one is immune to being spiritually drained. There are also medical emergencies and diseases at advanced stages that require a formal medical facility along with pharmaceutical treatment. In this case, energy healing can be used in conjunction as a secondary treatment.

Casting Out Spirits

Many times, you're unaware that the energy you're absorbing is negatively impacting your well-being. As spiritual awareness increases, you must seriously consider minimizing your exposure to harmful energy sources. This is prevention to protect your energy.

Manifested mental and physical imbalances are caused by spirits that trigger reactions that have already taken root. The causes of these health issues are also the cure if positioned at the opposite end of the energy spectrum. Once you're born, you're headed towards your death date. Intaking low-quality spirits accelerates the journey. The highest quality spirits sustain a healthy life.

Jesus demonstrated energy healing through the power of words, touch, and thoughts. This exemplifies your ability to radiate life-giving light with the vibrational power to move things. Every perceivable sign has an energy component. It's interesting to note that those in need of healing are referenced as unclean or demon-oppressed spirits. Unclean spirits refer to unhealthy habits expressed physically. Demon-oppressed spirits represent negative, self-inflicted thoughts and energy-draining emotions that destroy the physical body (like a form of mental illness).

Jesus was not addressing the flesh but instead focused on healing their spirit. However, he clearly noted the spirits in context as an illness, sickness, or impairment. This shows the importance of our soul being connected to the highest power for our well-being.

"Now there are a variety of gifts, but the same Spirit; and there are varieties of service, but the same Lord; and there are a variety of activities, but it is the same God who empowers them all in everyone... to another gifts of healing by the one Spirit ..." (1 Corinthians 12:4-9 ESV)

KEYNOTES | ENERGY HEALING

As the director of your energy, you are capable of being a healer. You can consume the highest quality energy to allow your system to repair itself and radiate positive light to provide an energy boost to others. Energy healing is restoration to healthy energy levels. You have power. Your strength is based on the spirits you've paid attention to and allowed to take root.

Spiritual Spark Exercise

Each day, continue to be more mindful of giving the body and mind the proper energy to stimulate self-healing. Pick a date on your calendar to honor your body, mind, and spirit with acts of self-preservation. Make a date with yourself and avoid distractions by placing your phone on DND. Provide your body with the highest quality nutrients possible and surround yourself with high-spirited individuals only. Participate in activities such as reading, writing, sitting quietly, resting, meditating, yoga, breath work, or any other exercise that elevates your awareness about the mind or body while simultaneously uplifting your energy.

CHAPTER 20

SELF-CARE ISN'T SELFISH

Boundaries Are Invisible Shields

Your decisions reflect the power of persuasion in your life. Unhealthy decisions are mostly made in moments of weakness. Protecting your energy is not a selfish act, it's self-preservation. You can pour into others when you have an overflow of energy. You do what you can when you are half-full. **If you are functioning on fumes, you have no energy to spare.** Anyone unwilling to respect your boundaries is selfish.

Not having enough time for self-care is an excuse. Surely, the creator of the universe made the duration of the day sufficient. You can allocate time—unless you've given control of your twenty-four-hour day to someone else. The ranking you assign to your quality of life should be your decision, which makes you accountable.

Activities are performed best with efficient physical, emotional, or mental strength. Giving away energy you don't have to spare can lead to energy depletion below healthy levels. Being willing to give someone a ride with a fuel gauge on empty will result in both parties being stranded. Focus on healing yourself first, then help when you're able.

Helping doesn't mean you are responsible for solving someone else's problem. If you have an excess of what they need, this can be an opportunity to give. Helping can also be in the form of uplifting others to realize their ability to help themselves. This may not be the help they had in mind, but it could still be beneficial. The inspiration might be the actual solution. Oftentimes, people are simply in a state of mind that restricts them from seeing they have multiple options to save themselves. You can offer a perspective from the outside looking in that they aren't able to access from the center of the situation.

Rest Is Required

Self-neglect to care for others may seem plausible. However, nothing is more worthy of your attention than your well-being. Your life is a priceless asset under your care. **How you maintain your health is a direct reflection of who you truly consider yourself to be, a measurement of self-worth, and the level of respect you have for your creator.** Making decisions that contribute to poor health conditions is a form of self-destruction.

> *"Do you not know that you are the temple of God and that the Spirit of God dwells in you? If anyone defiles*

the temple of God, God will destroy him. For the temple
of God is holy, which temple you are." (1 Corinthians
3:16-17 NKJV)

Taking on the weight of the world without having adequate strength to handle your own affairs can potentially activate the sympathetic nervous system. This triggers an acute stress response called fight-or-flight. This response is reserved for conditions that threaten your survival. However, you can have an overstimulated reaction to an event that isn't a real threat. When this occurs, a rush of adrenaline and noradrenaline are secreted throughout the body, causing several physiological changes to perform more strenuous activity than usual. This temporarily halts activities such as healing and digestion to exert this energy toward surviving imminent danger.

Stress is prevalent in our society and a factor in many diseases. Chronic stress can suppress innate and adaptive immune responses. The elevated level of cortisol increases the chances for infections and inflammation. This is the start of autoimmune diseases and chronic inflammatory disorders.

The leading cause of death is not a factor of old age. Non-communicable diseases (NCDs) such as cardiovascular disease, cancer, chronic respiratory diseases, diabetes, obesity, and cognitive impairment are among the leading causes of death and disability throughout the world. Unhealthy lifestyle contributors include malnutrition, unhealthy diet, smoking, alcohol consumption, drug abuse, stress, and overuse and misuse of technology.

Technology has its benefits and drawbacks. Everything has a soul (surrounding energy field) with spirit (radiation) energy emitted. Every electrical appliance in your home and your mobile devices emit radiofrequency electromagnetic fields (EMFs). Overuse and the layering of multiple EMFs from these electronics can produce toxic levels of radiation that interfere with the vibration of your EMF. This could alter your vibration to harmful levels. Adverse effects include nerve stimulation and an increase in body temperature.

Rest from energy-draining spirits throughout the day can provide a much-needed reset. Your entire system requires relaxation just as much as you need energy to do work. You can identify which activities and foods replenish or drain your energy by assessing your energy use. Then, you can make the necessary adjustments to include breaks to restore and maintain healthy energy levels. Optimal performance requires sufficient high-quality energy. A person with a drained spirit or health condition can still be useful to the spirit working through them, but partial potential is less than full capacity.

> "... let us cleanse ourselves from every defilement of body and spirit bringing holiness to completion ..."
> (2 Corinthians 7:1 ESV)

Self-investments Yield Abundance

"... I have come that they may have life, and that they may have it more abundantly." (John 10:10 NKJV)

Self-investing accumulates to a mindset of abundance as you continue repositioning yourself closer to God's unlimited power. It's basically investing a portion of your energy into yourself for the continuous elevation of consciousness. No other use of your resources has a greater rate of return than a healthy life. **Activities that push the mind and body beyond current limitations require stimulation from a power source that can surpass the strength of your current willpower.** You can't expect to successfully start and maintain new habits without the necessary mental strength. Doing so could be the downfall of many attempts.

Voluntary positive habits usually start in the mind by a personal decision to change. Changes induced by health scares are forced for survival. If possible, avoid making drastic lifestyle changes from a state of fear. Making a gradual transition toward a healthier lifestyle before the onset of symptoms or in the beginning stages of a problem can minimize the chance of anguish that often accompanies major lifestyle adjustments during a stressful period.

Practicing techniques for self-healing, spiritual recharging, and relaxation is an energy boost. Surface-level maintenance alone isn't very effective at improving your well-being. However, adding a mindful intention to any activity can increase the benefits of an experience.

Movement has magic to heal. It is the ultimate sign of life. Even a rock has energy and the ability to move. If you're moving toward the light, you become more radiant. Radiance is a sign of good health. So, at the very least, you could stimulate the mind with music while stretching the body for a few minutes every day.

Mindfulness can be as simple as consciously inhaling the force of life and exhaling any pent-up energy. You can increase energy flow with physical activity, breathing exercises, or the use of your vocal cords. Drinking water is also a great way to get things moving inside of you.

> *"Beloved, I pray that you may prosper in all things and be in health, just as your soul prospers." (3 John 1:2 NKJV)*

KEYNOTES | SELF-CARE ISN'T SELFISH

Putting the affairs of others before your own is self-neglect. Self-neglect indicates a weak will to commit to a self-care routine. To radiate positive light and pour into others, you must be physically and mentally able to do so. Your quality of life and the people you assist would benefit more from the healthier version of you.

Spiritual Spark Exercise

Using or hearing the word "no" shouldn't be dreaded. It's a word that can serve as a shield to protect your energy. Think of a past or present energy draining situation that could have, or can be, avoided by replying with "no." Replay the scenario in your mind. Get comfortable responding with "no." Don't substitute "no" with "maybe" or "I'll think about it," when the gut feeling is no. Just say "no." The word "no" can set protective boundaries without an explanation needed. If your "no" turns into a "yes" because you gained the capacity, then that's fine. It's more comfortable to turn "no" into "yes" versus "yes" into "no" once you've already relayed the message.

CHAPTER 21

OVERCOMING NEGATIVITY

Negative thought patterns and the concerns of what other people think of you are two of the most challenging barriers to overcome. However, they must be conquered to ascend as the higher self. Choosing to focus on or sharing negative information is not a reflection of one's higher self.

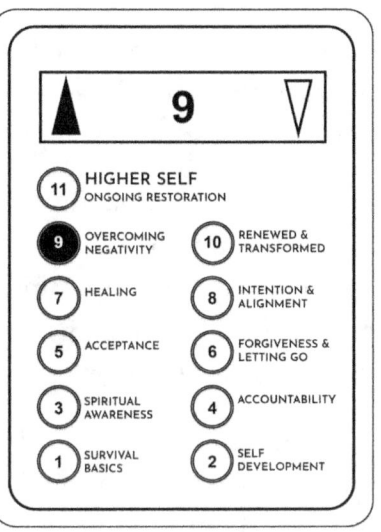

Negativity has been the roadblock for many. **Noticing negativity can be a reminder to stay focused.** Only a few people will muster the strength and confidence to rise above this obstacle. Once bypassed, the mind is liberated to excel to greatness. Then, consciousness becomes a sacred place.

To overcome negativity, you need to keep your mental storehouse fully stocked with a supply of truth. At the onset of negative information, you are ready to immediately replace it with positivity, so that it has minimal or no effect on your state of mind.

Someone exhibiting the behavior of a hater is reflecting their level of self-awareness. They are paying moments of their valuable life to engage in content that they claim to have no merit. They could be focusing on something they consider beneficial, but they are unconsciously choosing distractions. They have a right to voice their opinion, and you have a right to disregard them.

Why waste valuable time and energy by paying for negative information with your attention? Remember, your attention equates to moments of life. Your energy can be replenished, but the time spent using it can't be. Protect your energy by remaining focused on things that are worthy.

The only life you control is your own. How someone else decides to express themselves is their own business. When you feel the urge to be a hater or pay attention to a hater, you can refrain by redirecting your attention. You can redirect attention towards:

- Your life's intention
- Reframing the information as a message intended for growth or a reminder to stay focused
- Repeating a mantra or positive affirmation such as, "I decide what is worthy of my time and attention" or "I only focus on positive information and solutions"

- The impact of your contributions on the lives of the people you're meant to serve
- Your storehouse of spiritual truth
- Supportive friends, family, and colleagues
- The most inspirational person in your life, and imagine your world full of people with this persona encouraging you to continue to do what you do
- Empathy and compassion for the hater if they are impossible to disregard; and give thanks for them taking the time to recognize you exist and are doing something worthy of their attention (this can be a mental note and not an actual response to the person)

You only notice what you give attention to. You can use your assets constructively or destructively. After a while it will become uncomfortable to entertain sabotaging information. If negativity prevails, it's because you have allowed it. If this is the case, you should up the dosage of empowerment.

> "Set your mind on things above, not on things on the earth." (Colossians 3:2 NKJV)

Overcoming is having enough strength to get through, over, or past an obstacle. Being concerned about what others may think of you is a part of human nature. If you can get to the point where negativity appears as a speed bump rather than a barrier, it is no longer an obstacle.

Rising Above Daunting Spirits

You can unconsciously invite unwanted guests known as negative feelings. Just because they show up doesn't mean you have to let them stay. Energy draining emotions will occasionally pop up. All possible emotions are natural human responses. **Mental struggles can be viewed as spiritual strength training exercises.** The more you overcome, the stronger you become.

Your thoughts, the feelings you assign to them, and your actions are solely of your own doing. External conditions are not the cause. Although these conditions evoke a response, they are simply signs of something happening. You should be able to take full accountability for your response. Pointing the finger at others for provoking your behavior is admitting to a thoughtless auto-pilot reaction or that you lack self-control. The phrase "they made me do it" is not thinking from a high frame of mind.

Most people aren't aware of the constant transfer of energy or their energy's influence on the well-being of other people, while some people intentionally poke to get a reaction. If you can't express your emotions in a healthy manner, you should seek ways to calm your mind before interacting. It's inconsiderate to involve others in energy-draining circumstances unless they are willing to be involved to act as inspiration.

"Be completely humble and gentle; be patient, bearing with one another in love. Make every effort to keep

the unity of the Spirit through the bond of peace."
(Ephesians 4:2-3 NIV)

Energy-draining thought loops are a self-inflicted issue. You may replay a negative encounter numerous times in your mind. You haven't allowed the feelings to properly flow through because you've decided to handle it from a drained emotional state. This easily becomes a wild ride that you can't seem to get off, no matter how hard you try. When you finally snap out of it, those thoughts should be replaced with positive power thoughts or an activity that puts you in a higher frame of mind. Once you have calmed the mind, you can consider a better way to reframe the situation or talk to someone for a positive outlook.

"He gives power to the weak, And to those who have
no might He increases strength." (Isaiah 40:39 NKJV)

By rewriting the script of a negative experience, you can reprogram your behavioral reflex. The revised replay should show how you could have handled the situation in a positive manner. This is an effective self-healing approach to apply to any situation that you have processed in an unhealthy manner. It's pointing out your weakness and then imagining how things would unfold if you were strengthened in that area.

Considering the reaction of others involved is irrelevant. They are allowed to say and do as they please. Needing someone to apologize or respond a certain way before you can forgive or respond in a positive manner is allowing someone else to control your ability to move forward. This is about your growth. The growth of others is their own concern. Just because you want to change doesn't mean they are ready to do the same. You must accept their response as is and let it be.

Will the Way Regardless

"For if there is first a willing mind, it is accepted according to what one has, and not according to what he does not have." (2 Corinthians 8:12 NKJV)

We are quick to note the reasons why we can't do something. It's easy to list all the reasons why you can't do a thing. Some people don't realize this is a negative thinking pattern. **Thinking of reasons why you can't will not provoke inspiring thoughts of ways you can.**

Creating solutions is a vibration booster. You must focus on the positive to come up with reasons why you can. The question to yourself is, *How can I ...?* Then, it takes faith and imagination to visualize the assignment accomplished. In each moment, you are enough, and you have enough. God multiplies the strength of your light as you diligently seek to rise and surpass limitations.

"For whoever has, to him more will be given, and he will have abundance; but whoever does not have, even

what he has will be taken away from him." (Matthew 13:12 NKJV)

Reframing Lack or Loss

At the core of your being, you are energy. All darkness is a sign that there is a lack of light. Therefore, all lack derives from not being able to see the light in that area of your life. **All negative attributes can shift to the positive side when energy is restored.** Thoughts or conditions associated with loss or lack drain your energy.

If your focus is on things you lack, then it's not on the source of abundant power. Shift your focus to the highest power to boost your spirit and improve any areas of weakness. It's important to note that all currents are signs of energy flow. So, to see a change, you need a spirit with the power to move things in your favor.

Energy can't be lost or destroyed, but it can be transferred or transformed. Anything other than the bare substance of energy is impermanent and will cease to exist at some point. This includes you. You will witness things come and go beyond your control. The systems and cycles of existence are by nature's design. As thoughts of lack or loss creep in, rather than paying attention to something we can't control, we can turn our attention to something that raises our energy. The sun goes down daily, but it also rises again.

Forming Positive Thinking Patterns

Positive thinking is easier said than done. It's easy to get caught up or not even realize negative thought patterns. When you think about it, there are a lot of positive things going on in the universe. The sun, moon, stars, and Earth are still in formation. However, we tend to be laser-focused on the list of petty things that we don't have, what other people are doing wrong, and the most discouraging news.

You don't need to know about every trending crisis. Some of the conditions that currently trigger negative thoughts were once desires, and most people you complain about are reflecting qualities you have or had. You direct your attention to the things you notice and decide whether to stay tuned for more information. You can focus on the positive opposite.

Another negative thought pattern that may go unnoticed is speaking of unwanted conditions instead of what you do want. This directs your attention to the condition you are hoping to avoid. In this case, unpleasant memories may start to resurface rather than imagining your heart's desire being fulfilled. You can replace the negative words with the positive opposite. Instead of, "I don't want to experience another bad ..." you could say, "I want to experience a wonderful ..."

Assuming the worst of a situation is pessimistic. The worst that life has to offer can be a possibility with or without the use of your mental energy. Instead, you can ask and answer a question such as, "Given the conditions, how can I make the best of this situation?" Some solutions can be found in forming a question and then finding the answer.

Why not think of the best possible scenario as well? This can create positive synergy with all the moving parts. You don't need to stir unnecessary anxiety for something that may or may not happen. You can only do what you can do. It's unhealthy to hold yourself accountable for something beyond your control.

> *"Death and life are in the power of the tongue: and they that love it shall eat the fruit thereof." (Proverbs 18:21)*

Self-admiration

> *"There is one glory of the sun, another glory of the moon, and another glory of the stars; for one star differs from another star in glory." (1 Corinthians 15:41 NKJV)*

Each star is different, but they all exist to shine. Being the target or instigator of body shaming towards yourself or others is obviously a negative thought inducer. Everything about any of us is a part of our unique story. Just like the stars of a solar system, we all impact the lives around us.

Your energy can move the objects within your sphere of influence towards chaos or peace. Your visible and invisible attributes make you relatable to whomever you are meant to inspire.

You are responsible for the maintenance of your body, but genetics are outside of your control. You are not a visual display on the stage of the world for critique based on physical form. An inconceivable intelligence intricately designed each of us exactly as we are for a purpose greater than what's perceived by the eyes.

Honor your body as the divine gift that it is. You are created by God, in the image of God. Out of respect for your creator, have self-admiration and revere the light in all things made—regardless of someone else's opinion. The intelligence of your body is inconceivable and astonishing. A healthy mind and body are treasures that allow you to see the light of all things rather than featuring physical forms.

Judging

We have all fallen short of righteousness in countless ways. Who are we to judge? When you witness someone behaving in a senseless manner toward you or someone else, audit your own behavior to see where you may have conducted yourself in a similar way. No matter what you're going through (unless you have a mental disorder), it doesn't excuse rude or inappropriate behavior. If you are quick to pass judgement, it could be an indicator that you aren't as mature as you think you are.

Thinking from a higher state of consciousness is accompanied by empathy and compassion. You can't possibly imagine what it's like to live someone else's life. You can avoid saying the phrase "If it were me ..." because it's not and never will be. What you see of anyone's life is a glimpse. You can give your opinion, but at the same time, note your ignorance about the workings of another person's mind and the totality of their experience. This is also a reason why you shouldn't take other people's opinions about you personally. Only the Spirit of God can give the words that speak from knowing the totality of your being.

> *"And why do you look at the speck in your brother's eye, but do not consider the plank in your own eye?" (Matthew 7:3 NKJV)*

Acceptance and Letting Go

Learning to disregard negativity and distractions are a part of elevating your consciousness. You could learn to accept that other people will be opinionated about your life. You coexist in a world where everyone and everything is uniquely different. Conflicting views are inescapable. If what others say and think about you is a major concern, you need to find the strength to overcome the limitations set by unconsciously valuing the opinion of others more than you value truth.

Accepting others and your conditions as they are doesn't mean you should remain involved in unhealthy situations. Knowing when it's time to cut ties to people, places, and things is beneficial to your growth. Nothing is permanent. Good-bye, so long, and farewell aren't bad words. Letting go lightens the load as you prepare for takeoff into heavenly states of being.

> *"Be on your guard; stand firm in the faith; be courageous; be strong. Do everything in love." (1 Corinthians 16:13-14 NIV)*

KEYNOTES | OVERCOMING NEGATIVITY

You have your own life to live. You don't have to accept the opinions of others. You decide what to focus on. There is so much beauty and positivity in the world. The universe has an unfathomable size, but we often focus on petty things that don't deserve our attention. Unnecessarily absorbing spirits that drain our energy is a self-sabotaging act. If your mind is taunting you, it's a sign that you need to move closer to light. This includes eliminating distractions to increase your focus on strengthening yourself. Retreating from certain social activities may be beneficial. You must gauge the things in your life to determine which aspects support your intentions. To continue rising, you must continuously detach from the perspective that's holding you down.

Spiritual Spark Exercise

Make the decision to focus only on the positive. If there is someone or something stopping you from living your best life right now, immediately go look in the mirror and tell yourself, "I free myself from the delusion that other people or things have power over me. I invite the highest power to be my shield while working on me and through me."

CHAPTER 22

APPOINTED, QUALIFIED, AND GIFTED BY THE SPIRIT

God's Plan

> *"Who shall bring a charge against God's elect? It is God who justifies." (Romans 8:33 NKJV)*

The attributes of the spirits you absorb work through you in all that you do. If you are appointed by God, then you are also qualified by this power. You don't need approval from other people to pursue an assignment from God. **Worldly certifications can be useful, but truth students are taught by the spirit of the highest power.** The necessary skills and resources are acquired along your path. There isn't an official plan when you're under the direct inspiration of God's plan.

> *"You did not choose Me, but I chose you and appointed you that you should go and bear fruit, and that your fruit should remain, that whatever you ask the Father in My name He may give you." (John 15:16 NKJV)*

187

We Aren't Rats in a Race

The average person spends most of their waking hours providing a service to earn income. The impact a career has on your well-being and lifestyle should be of utmost concern. At a certain point in life, you should be in the position to find or create work that supports your well-being and desired lifestyle, versus being subjected to employment with unfavorable terms. The life you want to live is a possible reality. Once you have set an intention, your work should align with it.

Being a vessel for God, seems to be secondary nature for many, if considered at all. The attitude of working to pay the bills is essentially working for money. Money shouldn't be the primary incentive. **Your role should also contribute toward strengthening your mind, improving your circumstances, and being a positive light to those you serve.** All positions deposit information required for future use. Every part of your life communicates a message. Life isn't meant to be a repeat of yesterday. Invest a portion of your energy to lift you higher. By doing so, you gradually transform your life.

There aren't many people joyfully proclaiming a higher power is working through them in their current position. Instead, some jobs are described as stressful, draining, or unfulfilling. Which is probably why so many are feeling stuck in their current occupation. Some people can't imagine the ideal life they want without applying the restrictions of current circumstances to future projections.

Imagination is unlimited. It's the place where you should see yourself in perfect health with all possibilities as an option. The circumstances already exist. Imagination is the tool to go from current circumstances to where you want to be. The imagination is a spiritual signal that the ideal position is attainable.

> *"Moreover whom He predestined, these He also called; whom He called, these He also justified; and whom He justified, these He also glorified." (Roman 8:30 NKJV)*

Your actions are predestined by the qualities of the spirits that influence your mind. In other words, your actions are first performed in the mind, where you may witness them as imagination. The spirit pervading your mind and body gives the command, and then you react. The energy characteristics of the spirits you absorb are transmitted to you. **If your willpower isn't strong enough to help you achieve your goals, you need to put more effort into absorbing the traits from qualified spirits that will move you forward.**

The spirit goes before you at the speed of light to determine the way and swiftly returns with a step-by-step guide. Living in each moment and trusting the next step will unfold as you take it, can preserve your energy from being drained by anxiety. There are many steps involved in complex assignments. You get glimpses in segments to continue moving forward. You might not live to see its completion, but you can live to walk in that direction.

Imagination is the faculty of predestination. To physically arrive at the destination, you must follow the steps you are given. Entertaining opposing spirits is not one of the steps. Your spiritual resources can work in your favor if you know how to use them. You have the faculty of consciousness to co-create the life you want. **Feeling stuck could be a sign that you have been given the next step, but you haven't taken it because you're wanting to see the entire staircase prematurely.**

You may begin to feel uninspired if you have outgrown your current role. It may be time to consider an assignment based on who you are today, not who you were when you applied. You must determine when it's time to let go, move up, or move on.

You don't lose what is divinely yours. The skills and mental growth gained from each position will transfer into the next appointed assignment. The position you leave behind is the appointed role for the person meant to fill it. Don't hinder your growth by being overly concerned or overestimating your impact on your employer's stability.

Your resignation shouldn't cause someone else's company to collapse if it's structured properly. Trust that they will find a way to progress as you find yours. It may be the best move for both parties. Moving on and moving up is a positive move if you see the situation in the right light.

You are made in the image of God. Therefore, you have an innate desire to be creative. If your current job doesn't offer advancement opportunities that allow you to demonstrate your capabilities, moving on seems to be the best option to further advance. You shouldn't wait for opportunities to present themselves. You can take the initiative to find the niche that you could apply yourself to and add value.

> *"And whatever you do, do it heartily, as to the Lord and not to men, knowing that from the Lord you will receive the reward of the inheritance; for you serve the Lord Christ." (Colossians 3:23-24 NKJV)*

On-the-job Stress Costs More Than You're Paid

It's possible that unfavorable work conditions are a result of your own doing. You could be making assumptions about the expectations of your role. Failure to effectively communicate an issue sends a message that there is no issue. Even if there is a known issue, if the people involved don't voice their opinions, it may not appear as a priority.

You exchange moments of your life to earn an income. No form of work is worth putting your health at risk. If your health is declining due to work-related stress, you must consider all options to make health a priority. This could be difficult when considering financial responsibilities. In this case, you must remember who you are with unwavering faith.

Some situations call for you to act before seeing physical signs of how things will develop. This is a true demonstration of faith. The Spirit of God provides the strength to conquer all circumstances, but it requires faith and action on your part to apply it effectively. To do God's will, you must take the step. If the qualities of God's spirit are powering your being, it is also powering your imagination. You envision possibilities related to where you are in the moment and what can occur if you stay tuned to the level of spirits providing that projection.

> *"But without faith it is impossible to please Him, for he who comes to God must believe that He is, and that He is a rewarder of those who diligently seek Him." (Hebrews 11:6 NKJV)*

You can't afford to ignore the distress call of your body. If you aren't willing to take time out to prevent a health complication, you may be forced to take time off for a necessary treatment and recovery period. If you are neglecting your health, you should strongly consider your reasons for doing so. Work-related factors are at the top of the list for causing stress.

Fulfilling your purpose does not come at the expense of your health. God could still use you during or after a health issue. However, you don't have to subject yourself to harmful situations as an act of gratitude (or from a state of fear) for a position that's killing you.

> *"For God hath not given us the spirit of fear; but of power, and of love, and of a sound mind." (2 Timothy 1:7)*

KEYNOTES | APPOINTED, QUALIFIED, AND GIFTED BY THE SPIRIT

You are enough exactly as you are. Your powering source determines your will and provides the commands that trigger your reactions. It's important that you're tuned into spirits with the authority to qualify, appoint, and reveal your innate gifts. If you are powered by God, there isn't a higher authority.

God's plan is laid out step by step for you to follow. You can't see the information and connections that will be gained as you progress. Therefore, mapping out the entire way shouldn't be your concern. Remain laser-focused on performing the present step to the best of your ability. It activates the link for the next step to manifest.

If you trust the process and follow your inner guide, you can materialize the projected future of your imagination. Clear visualization of your next step indicates readiness to take it. Your unique staircase is designed by a series of electrical impulses which you sense as thoughts of inspiration.

Spiritual Spark Exercise

If you're ready to radiate your brightest light, with the next idea you receive from God, act on it. Then continue to do so for the rest of your life.

CHAPTER 23

RADIATING RENEWED LIGHT

"For as we have many members in one body, but all the members do not have the same function, so we, being many, are one body in Christ, and individually members of one another." (Romans 12:4-5 NKJV)

The Spirit is the single force that permeates everything, connecting us all as one. Empowered by the Spirit of God, you perceive the same world with a renewed mind, a healthier body, and a restored soul, all from a different perspective. The focus is shifted from physical attributes to recognizing the spirit of things. Your intention redirects your attention toward maintaining your light in alignment with your desires and inspirations. Physical attributes are pertinent descriptions for identification, but your spirit works to present the qualities of the highest light.

Through the process of self-realization, you have taken your experiences into spiritual account by seeing all circumstances with the perspective of light. You are continuously surpassing the invisible ceiling created by the limitations of your mind.

Life is shaped by both personal and universal moves, influenced by the interactions of spirits. Your new perspective under the influence of God's Spirit allows you to see the light of God in all things. This can only be achieved by your love for God. If your mind can be renewed, so can the minds of others.

In life, you get the hand you're dealt, not the one you choose. You were born into circumstances that may not be ideal. However, you do get to choose your own adventure when it comes to how you respond and the spirit you emit. Despite what you have gone through, or maybe going through, you have the power within you to overcome it. You always were and forever will be the light of the world. Now is the time to rise like the sun and embrace your position as a shining star!

> *"Yet in all these things we are more than conquerors through Him who loved us. For I am persuaded that neither death nor life, nor angels nor principalities nor powers, nor things present nor things to come, nor height nor depth, nor any other created thing, shall be able to separate us from the love of God which is in Christ Jesus our Lord." (Romans 8:37-39)*

KEYNOTES | RADIATING RENEWED LIGHT

You are a spiritual spark. May all that you do occur gracefully with divine perfection. Claim your inherited power and be mindful of the influential spirits of all things. Protect your energy, recharge, and radiate your renewed light.

Spiritual Spark Exercise

Take a moment to appreciate and reflect on the nature of your inner light. Then go out and shine it into the world!

REMEMBERING I AM ...

Affirmations with Bible References

- "... born again, a new creation. The old has passed away; behold, the new has come" (2 Corinthians 5:17)
- created in the image of God (Genesis 1:27; Ephesians 4:24)
- healed (Isaiah 53:5; 1 Peter 2:24)
- not alone. The power of God is with me. (Isaiah 41:10)
- one with God (1 Corinthians 6:17)
- "... not given the spirit of fear; but of power, and of love, and of a sound mind" (2 Timothy 1:7)
- "... the light of the world ..." (Matthew 5:14)
- what I am by the grace of God (1 Corinthians 15:10)
- "... rooted and grounded in love" (Ephesians 3:17)

- filled with all the fullness of God (Ephesians 3:19)

- pressing toward the mark for the prize of the high calling of God in Christ Jesus (Philippians 3:14)

- chosen, appointed, and given what I ask by God (John 15:16)

- an ambassador for God (2 Corinthians 5:20)

- "… taught by the Spirit, interpreting Spiritual Truths to those who are spiritual" (1 Corinthians 2:13)

- "… given the manifestation of the Spirit for the common good" (1 Corinthians 12:7)

- able to do all things through Him who strengthens me (Philippians 4:13)

- perfect for my purpose just as I am (2 Corinthians 8:10-12)

- God's workmanship created for good works, which God prepared beforehand, that I walk in them (Ephesians 2:10)

- the temple of the living God (2 Corinthians 6:16)

- God's temple and God's Spirit dwells in me (1 Corinthians 3:16)

- born again, not of perishable seed but of imperishable, through the living and abiding word of God (1 Peter 1:23)

- the head and not the tail, and I only go up and not down in life as I trust and obey the commands of God (Deuteronomy 28:13)
- greatly loved by God (John 3:16; Ephesians 2:4; 1 Thessalonians 1:4)
- "... the elect of God" (Colossians 3:12)
- "strengthened with all might, according to His glorious power ..." (Colossians 1:11)
- called by the grace of God (2 Timothy 1:9)
- a friend of God (John 15:15)
- God's fellow worker (1 Corinthians 3:9)

BIBLIOGRAPHY:

1. Cleveland Clinic. Serotonin. Last reviewed on 3/18/2022. https://my.clevelandclinic.org/health/articles/22572-serotonin

2. Slominski AT, Zmijewski MA, Plonka PM, Szaflarski JP, Paus R. How UV Light Touches the Brain and Endocrine System Through Skin, and Why. Endocrinology. 2018 May 1;159(5):1992-2007. doi: 10.1210/en.2017-03230. PMID: 29546369; PMCID: PMC5905393. https://pmc.ncbi.nlm.nih.gov/articles/PMC5905393/

3. Gamble KL, Berry R, Frank SJ, Young ME. Circadian clock control of endocrine factors. Nat Rev Endocrinol. 2014 Aug;10(8):466-75. doi: 10.1038/nrendo.2014.78. Epub 2014 May 27. PMID: 24863387; PMCID: PMC4304769.

4. EPA, United States Environmental Protection Agency. Overview of the Endocrine System. The endocrine system, made up, the metabolism and blood sugar. https://www.epa.gov/endocrine-disruption/overview-endocrine-system

5. Benavidez GA, Zahnd WE, Hung P, Eberth JM. Chronic Disease Prevalence in the US: Sociodemographic and

Geographic Variations by Zip Code Tabulation Area. Original Research, Volume 21, February 29, 2024. Prev Chronic Dis 2024; 21:230267. DOI: https://www.cdc.gov/pcd/issues/2024/23_0267.htm

6. Morris AL, Mohiuddin SS. Biochemistry, Nutrients. [Updated 2023 May 1]. In: StatPearls [Internet]. Treasure Island (FL): StatPearls Publishing; 2025 Jan-. Available from: https://www.ncbi.nlm.nih.gov/books/NBK554545/

ABOUT THE AUTHOR

K ali Denise is a radiant light appointed by the Spirit to rise. She is fully committed to the works inspired by spiritual truth. *Radiating Renewed Light* is her first book, written as she commences the roles associated with reflecting the highest power. She is a dedicated channel to receive the interpretation of spiritual truth. She considers herself an ordinary person with a keen awareness of her energy from the extraordinary light of God's heavenly power.